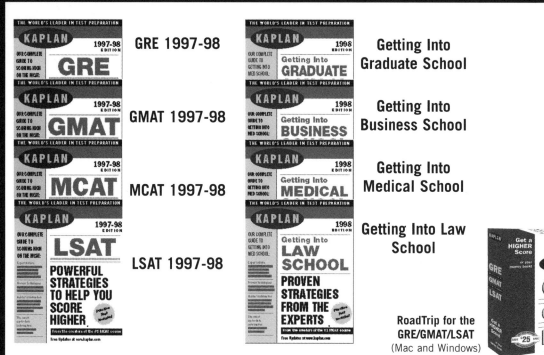

KAPLAN®

GOING INDIE:

Self-Employment, Freelance, and Temping Opportunities

by Kathi Elster
and Katherine Crowley

Published by
Kaplan Educational Centers and Simon & Schuster
1230 Avenue of the Americas
New York, NY 10020

Special thanks to Doreen Beauregard and Evelyn Lontok.

Project Editor: Donna Ratajczak
Production Editor: Maude Spekes
Layout Design: gumption design
Production Coordinator: Gerard Capistrano
Managing Editor: Kiernan McGuire
Executive Editor: Del Franz

Manufactured in the United States of America
Published Simultaneously in Canada
March 1997

Library of Congress Cataloging-in-Publication Data

Elster, Kathi.
Going indie: self-employment, freelance, and temping opportunities / by Kathi Elster and Katherine Crowley.
p. cm.
Includes bibliographical references.
ISBN 0-684-83756-0
1. Self-employed. I. Crowley, Katherine. II. Title.
HD8036.E47 1997
658'.041--dc21 97-3406
CIP

CONTENTS

ABOUT THE AUTHORS

Kathi Elster

Kathi Elster is an expert on the topic of small business ownership. Through her business support program, The Business Strategy Seminar, Kathi has helped thousands of entrepreneurs launch their ideas and grow their businesses. Ms. Elster is also an adjunct professor at Baruch College and the New School in New York City.

Katherine Crowley

A partner in The Business Strategy Seminar, Katherine Crowley is a former employment counselor and a Harvard-trained psychotherapist. Ms. Crowley is an expert on the psychology of small business ownership and self-employment.

This book is dedicated to Irving Krieger,
a man who embodied the indie spirit and passed it on to all who knew him.

ACKNOWLEDGMENTS

We gratefully acknowledge...

All the members of Kaplan staff who recognized the value of our information and encouraged us, especially Jay Johnson, Del Franz, and Donna Ratajczak.

We also acknowledge Carol Crowley for her contribution to the title of this book and her indie vision; Thelma Krieger for her belief in us and constant encouragement; John Crowley for his interest, assurance, and support; Bee Winkler for her enthusiastic response to our early drafts; David Winkler for his constant ear, patience, and undying faith.

Finally, we'd like to acknowledge all of our clients. The risks that you take are a constant source of inspiration to us. Thank you for your ongoing, courageous efforts to make your work and your lifestyles fulfilling.

We specifically want to thank those who contributed directly to our indie profiles: Neville Bean, Robin Kormos, Blair Wijnkoop, Alice Simpson, Bernadette Kathryn, Susan Steiger, Sarah Brezavar, John Follis, Denise Caruso, Stefan Killen, Suzanne Swift, Robert Gould, Julia Kasolapova, Belinda Clarke, Karen Frankfeldt, Shimoda, and Robert Agee.

section 1

welcome to the INDIE REVOLUTION

chapter 1
INTRODUCTION

If you're thinking of "going indie," you could be on the verge the smartest career move of your life. The job market of the nineties and the next millennium belongs to indies—*independent individuals* who take sole responsibility for generating their income and directing their careers. An indie might be classified as a temp, a part-time worker, a freelance consultant, or a business owner. The common denominator is *self*-employment. In one way or another, indies are out there on their own, selling their services and products in the marketplace.

Over the last 12 years, we've worked with more than 10,000 indies from every industry. We've run hundreds of seminars and support groups for small-business owners. We've taught the skills for "going indie" at local colleges, national conferences, and professional trade associations. We've counseled individuals through the emotional and psychological challenges of self-employment. Through our classes, seminars, support groups, lectures, and consultations, we've helped thousands of individuals discover their indie career paths.

In our contact with newcomers to the indie revolution, we've noticed that certain questions come up again and again. The purpose of this book is to answer those questions to help you begin forging your indie career today. We'll be covering everything you want to know about starting an indie venture. We'll also tell you the things you don't know that you need to know. Our aim is to dispel the myths that prevent talented people like you from going indie.

> "The modern world is on the verge of another huge leap in creativity and productivity, but the traditional job is not going to be part of tomorrow's economic reality. There still is and will always be enormous amounts of work to do, but it is not going to be contained in the familiar envelopes we call jobs. In fact, many organizations are today well along the path toward being de-jobbed."
>
> —William Bridges,"The End Of The Job," *Fortune,* September 19, 1994.

FREQUENTLY ASKED QUESTIONS ABOUT GOING INDIE

1. How do I know what kind of business to go into?

If you're like most people, you don't. Choosing a business opportunity takes research and careful self-examination. This

> "Risk and responsibility have been redefined: The good job, once the definition of responsibility, is now a very risky business, and the old kind of freelance activity that was once risky is now in tune with the future and is becoming the choice of many people who want to act responsibly."
>
> —William Bridges, "The End Of The Job," *Fortune,* September 19, 1994.

book will coach you through the process. In chapters 5, 6, 7, and 8 you'll find self-assessment exercises to pinpoint your talents, skills, interests, and lifestyle preferences. In chapter 9, you'll learn about business trends and 101 hot indie business ideas. In chapter 10, you'll put all of this information together to find your own indie profile. Chapter 11 explains how to test your indie business idea before making a full-time commitment—so you can look before you leap into self-employment.

2. How will I survive financially?

Financial independence is scary, but it's a fact of indie life. Temps, part-time workers, freelance consultants, and business owners are not like traditional employees. They can't rely on weekly paychecks and full-time benefits. As an indie, you have to shift from a paycheck mentality (someone pays you) to a payroll mentality (you pay yourself).

To make it as an indie, you'll need to learn new money management skills. Chapter 19 covers essential financial planning for your independent venture—everything from determining the cost of running your indie business to ensuring there will be money left over for your personal expenses.

3. Isn't it risky to be an indie?

Honestly, yes. In some respects going indie is riskier than being a traditional employee. You won't have the security of a regular paycheck, and you'll have to take risks as you pursue your own business idea. Balance the risk against the freedom to design a work life that fits you personally and professionally. Weigh the steady paycheck against unlimited earning potential. To win these personal and financial benefits, you must be willing to take risks. In chapter 14, we'll show you how other indies have managed their risks. You'll also have a chance to rate yourself as a risk taker.

4. Why do so many indie businesses fail?

The Department of Labor has been telling us that 80 percent of all small businesses fail. Here's why we believe that this statistic is incomplete and distorted.

- Most indie businesses do not "fail" outright; rather, the entrepreneur gives up and closes the business by choice.
- The Labor Department looks at only small businesses that have been incorporated. Many indie businesses are not incorporated and don't show up in government statistics.
- Freelancers, temps, and part-time workers are left out of the equation.

For these reasons, government studies do not necessarily report accurate success rates for independent business ventures. Among the indies we've worked with, we see a 50 percent success rate—much better odds.

5. If I'm an indie, how do I stay motivated?

When you're self-employed, your success depends upon your ability to stay motivated. For a crash course in the essential skill of self-management, turn to Chapter 12. Find out how to organize your work, manage your time, and coach yourself through obstacles.

6. I don't know how to sell my product or service to others. Can't I just hire someone to do it for me?

No. At least not at the beginning. The most important interpersonal skill for every indie is the ability to bring in the business. That means that if you're a temp, you'll need to pursue the best temp positions. If you're a part-time worker, you'll need to seek out the best part-time gigs. If you work freelance, you'll need to target the companies that offer the best returns for your skills. If you own a business, you'll have to find customers and sell your product or service to them. Read chapters 14 and 15 to learn about the basics of marketing and sales.

7. How do I know if I'll succeed?

The best answer to this question is that you'll have to believe in your success. And you'll have to be willing to do whatever it takes to make your indie venture happen. Successful indies share certain attitudes and behaviors that we'll explore in detail in chapter 2. We'll also tell you how to develop these traits in yourself now.

Because there are fewer traditional jobs, the greatest opportunities for interesting and rewarding work are available to indies—those independent individuals who take sole responsibility for generating their income and directing their careers. As an indie, you can create your own job as a temp, a freelance consultant, a part-time worker, or a business owner. Your first task will be to define your skills, explore your interests, and decide what indie business idea makes sense for you.

> More than 43 million jobs have been eliminated in the United States since 1979. Openings for traditional positions that were available to your parents and grandparents are decreasing. This trend will continue to shape the job market into the next millennium.
>
> —Louis Uchitelle and N.R. Kleinfield, "On the Battlefields of Business, Millions of Jobs Lost," *New York Times,* March 3, 1996

This book takes you step by step through the process of choosing the right business idea. It shows you how to master the essential skills and attitudes that'll bring you indie success for years to come. Welcome to the indie revolution!

Say Good Bye To . . .	Say Hello To . . .
A traditional job	The indie career path
A regular paycheck	Pay-per-job
A ceiling on your earnings	Unlimited earning potential
An employer defining your job	You defining your job
A company dress code	You deciding what to wear
A boss supervising your work	You supervising your work
Paid sick days and vacation	You pay for sick days and vacation
A boss scheduling your time	Scheduling your own time
Employer-paid health insurance	You buy health insurance
Using the company's office supplies	You supply the supplies
Listening to coworkers gripe	Dealing with isolation
The corporate work environment	Your own work environment
Commuting to work	Working where you want

chapter 2
SELF-EMPLOYMENT OPTIONS

While traditional jobs come in packages of more or less the same shape, self-employment can take many forms. As we discussed in the introduction, self-employment might mean working as a temp, a freelance consultant, or running your own business. Self-employment can even mean working full time within a company, but an indie job within a company will be project-based and flexible, not rigidly defined. "Going indie" means that you view yourself as an independent company, no matter what form of self-employment you're engaged in.

Indies have an attitude. The indie perspective on work and career is fundamentally different from the attitude of traditional job holders. Unlike employees, who rely on companies to define their jobs and give them financial security, indies accept that job security lies in their own ability to generate different kinds of work.

MORE GUTS, MORE GLORY

Compared to traditional jobs, indie jobs require more risk taking and more personal responsibility. Your *job*, if you work for a company, is flexible and constantly changing. You may be hired as a *temp* or a *part-time employee*. You may *telecommute* (work for a company from your home). If so, instead of going to the office, you're home alone. You communicate with your employer via computer, fax, and telephone.

Whatever kind of indie job you take, your work will require three essential behaviors:

1. Managing your own time
2. Prioritizing your own work
3. Pursuing new work opportunities on an ongoing basis

Some Indie Options

a. running your own business

b. getting hired as a temp

c. working part time

d. becoming a consultant

e. taking on freelance assignment

f. working full time for a company

g. some combination of options a–f

The country's largest employer, sending out 767,000 substitute workers each year, is Manpower Inc., the temporary help agency.

New York Times

Here's a brief introduction to all the ways that you can "go indie." Check out the different kinds of indie employment, and decide which one appeals to you.

TEMPING

Temps are individuals who get hired by temporary agencies for specific kinds of work. The agency takes responsibility for finding you short-term work assignments with companies that need your particular expertise. Your salary consists of an hourly wage paid by the temp agency. Temp agencies do not usually provide benefits, and they are not obligated to find you work. Savvy indies register with several agencies to see which one produces the best assignments.

Temp agencies now hire an incredibly wide range of temporary workers: graphic designers, technical writers, computer programmers, paralegals, proofreaders, textile and clothing designers, architects, accountants, medical professionals—you name it. Temping is an excellent way to build your skills while learning about your industry. It's not surprising that temping is one of the fastest growing sectors of the indie job market.

Maureen D. always loved word processing and designing graphics on her desktop computer. In college, Maureen registered with several temp agencies so she could make some extra money doing word processing at night. She got assignments at various publishing companies, typing book copy on the graveyard shift. Maureen became a regular temp at one of the educational publishing companies. Eventually, she was given the opportunity to assist with the layout and graphic design of several textbooks.

After graduation, Maureen continued to do temp work. This time, she registered with agencies that placed temporary graphic designers. With each assignment, Maureen learned a new brand of software, and completed another design assignment. After two years of temping, Maureen had developed a hefty portfolio of design work. She felt ready to start her own graphic design company.

PART-TIME WORK

Another popular option among indies is part-time work. Part-time jobs require 20 hours of work per week or fewer, on-site within a specific company. You may be a multitask worker with a variety of responsibilities. Part-time workers are usually paid by the hour or by the day. Most part-timers don't receive company benefits, although there are exceptions to the rule.

Like temping, part-time work is an excellent avenue for building skills and learning more about a given industry. Many indies take part-time jobs while they develop their own business ideas. Others take part-time work as waitresses, telemarketers, sales reps, or clerical staff so that they can have flexible hours while they pursue a bigger dream.

> Ever since high school, **Hugh G.** knew he wanted to design and sell his own software products. He also knew, however, that inventing, packaging, and distributing software products would take time. He had to find investors, write a business plan, and create prototypes of his software. Meanwhile, he relied on part-time work to pay the bills.
>
> Hugh found a part-time job as a technical support person for a major software company. Working five-hour shifts three days a week, Hugh fielded user questions and solved problems involving the company's software products. Hugh liked his job because as he assisted people with their problems, he learned which ingredients were the keys to effective software. In addition to his hourly wage, Hugh also gained invaluable information for his future indie business.

FREELANCE WORK

You might start your indie career as a freelancer. Freelancers hire out their expertise in some area on a project basis. The employer assumes that a freelancer will be able to complete the assignment with little or no supervision. Freelancers may be paid hourly or per project. They usually establish an hourly or daily rate for their expertise.

As a freelancer, you're responsible for cultivating your own client base. Each freelance "client" gives you a short-term assignment sealed with a contract that spells out the terms of the project—what you'll do and how you'll be paid. Although freelancers may work within companies, it is their responsibility to manage their own time and prioritize their work.

Jim G. is a freelance copywriter with a client base of small-to medium-sized companies. Jim's specialties include brochures, catalogs, annual reports, and promotional pieces. Some of Jim's clients hire him to work on the company premises. Others prefer he work at home. Jim finds his clients through professional networking events and word of mouth. When a potential freelance assignment comes in, Jim assesses the time it will take him to complete it. He then schedules that time into his week, around his other freelance assignments.

"Today's organization is rapidly being transformed from a structure built out of traditional jobs into a field of work needing to be done."

—William Bridges,"The End Of The Job," *Fortune,* September 19, 1994.

PROJECT-BASED EMPLOYMENT

Some indies choose project-based full-time employment. This form of indie work involves a short-term full-time commitment to a specific company. You are hired to work on a particular project. When the project ends, your job ends. Some indies go from project to project within the same company. Others prefer short stints at different companies.

Joseph H., a computer programmer, has an indie job in a bank. Joseph's job involves moving from project to project within the bank. Each computer programming project takes between four to six weeks to complete. When Joseph finishes one project, he's immediately assigned to the next one. Joseph's hours vary. For certain projects, he works from 4 P.M. to midnight. For others, he has a regular nine to five schedule. The late shifts are no problem for Joseph, because he gets paid a higher rate during evening hours.

BUSINESS OWNERSHIP

Some indies have a product or service that they want to sell to specific populations. They establish their own company, set sales goals, and write and follow a business plan. Indie business owners (also called *entrepreneurs*) take responsibility for all phases of running a business—from planning to sales to billing to customer relations.

Entrepreneurs set their own prices, work their own hours, and find their own customers. They pay themselves a salary from the net income of their business.

Jean W. runs an industrial cleaning service. She got the idea for her business while working as a part-time secretary at several companies. Jean noticed how poorly maintained many offices were, and decided she could make money offering low-cost, reliable cleaning.

To generate business, Jean puts ads in the local paper. She has a listing in the yellow pages, and keeps a file on all the inquiries she gets from prospective customers. In addition to selling her service, Jean hires and manages her cleaning crews. She also keeps track of her business' finances. She maintains accurate financial records and bills her customers regularly.

Customer satisfaction is a high priority for Jean. "If anyone complains, I address the problem immediately," she says. It's easy to see why Jean has established a sparkling reputation among her customers. Jean enjoys being her own boss. As she works on growing her company, her biggest challenge is keeping her own office clean!

Indie Option	Salary	Hours/Week	Work Place	Supervision	How to Find This Option
Temp	hourly	no more than 40	on-site at company	company boss	agencies
Part time	hourly	20 or fewer	on-site at company	company boss	newspaper agencies contacts
Freelance	hourly or daily	varies	on-site or at home	none	agencies contacts
Project	project fee	varies	on-site or	none at home	agencies contacts
Business	any combination	60+	your choice	none	your efforts

THREE INDIE CAREER TRACKS

Whether you have an indie job or you run a small business, be prepared for constant change. The information revolution has created an environment of continuous invention, innovation, and fluctuation. The indie job market is flourishing precisely because an independent enterprise can shift gears faster than a behemoth corporation. The better you are at adapting to changes in the marketplace, the more stability you will experience in your career. Stability at work now lies in flexibility.

The indie journeys described below will show you what we mean.

From architect to product designer . . .

After **John Q.** got a degree in architecture from Princeton University, he first looked for full-time work in an architecture firm. Although John did accept a position as an entry-level employee at a very prestigious architecture firm, he had already noticed that the architecture wasn't growing. John started looking for other ways to use his skills.

During his free time, John began to experiment with product design. He sold his first watch design to a watch manufacturing company. Within six months, John obtained four more product design assignments. By the end of the year, he quit his job at the architecture firm, and officially declared himself a full-time product designer.

From baby-sitter to children's center owner . . .

During college, **Janice S.** worked part time as a nanny for one of her professors. Janice always enjoyed working with kids, and the money helped with college expenses.

Armed with a teaching degree, Janice landed a full-time job teaching fourth graders. Three nights a week, Janice still provided child care for a two-child family. Moonlighting as a nanny supplemented her teaching income, and gave her more experience with kids.

Two years later, Janice was ready to make a change. She turned her full-time teaching job into a part-time job. She used her afternoon hours to plan and launch an after-school program for young children at the local YWCA. Within six months, the program took off, and Janice's reputation as a child activity expert grew.

After two more years, Janice took the big leap into business ownership. She left her teaching job altogether and started her own indie venture—a children's activity center that featured after-school programs and weekend events for parents and children.

From public relations intern to direct-mail company owner . . .

As a college senior, David M. interned at a public relations agency in the marketing department. That same agency hired David immediately after graduation to work on a six-month project involving direct mail.

David's next job was part time: two days a week in the production department of a direct mail company. Needing more money, David started working two more days a week as a writer for an advertising agency.

David juggled his part-time jobs for three years, learning about the direct mail industry and honing his writing skills. With this experience under his belt, David was eventually able to launch his own direct mail advertising company. He started his indie venture slowly, dropping the part-time writing job first while he built a solid client base. After one more year, David had accumulated enough clients to focus full time on his own business.

INDIE GROUND RULES

There are certain facts of independent life that hold true, whatever option you choose.

Indie jobs demand a different set of skills than those needed in traditional jobs.

The traditional job market rewarded employees for traits such as loyalty, dependability, and conformity—for following the rules. The typical company was a large organization with a well-defined hierarchy. If you performed your specific duties, did whatever the company told you to do without questioning authority, you were deemed a good worker.

In the information age, these traditional job behaviors are obsolete. Because companies need to adapt and react quickly, the qualities that are now prized are flexibility, ingenuity, and ability to take risks. Indies—whether they are part-time workers, temps, telecommuters, freelancers, or entrepreneurs—must practice a different set of personal and interpersonal skills from their counterparts in traditional jobs.

Indies need to know how to manage their own time, make good decisions, take risks, and produce results. They need to be flexible, creative, adaptable. They must be willing to market themselves to potential employers or customers. They need to set goals and develop plans for moving their careers forward. We will spend a good portion of this book describing the indie skill base, and showing you how to cultivate these abilities in yourself.

Looking for and acquiring work becomes an important, ongoing activity.

As we discussed, indie jobs are more temporary and project based than traditional jobs. An indie job may last one or two years. Freelance clients may last six months to a year. When the indie job or freelance assignment ends, you've got to secure new assignments. If you start your own business, you will always need to generate new customers. Every form of self-employment necessitates ongoing marketing and sales. We will discuss this topic in much greater detail in later chapters.

Defining your skills and abilities effectively becomes crucial.

Your ability to describe what you do, how well you do it, *and how you will benefit whoever hires you is more important than ever.* Today's résumés look more and more like small-business marketing materials. Individuals (*indie*-viduals) understand that today's employers want to know what value any new person will add to their company. The indie job market shifts the emphasis of looking for work from "What am I going to get?" to "What results am I going to create?"

EXAMPLES OF TRADITIONAL JOBS	EXAMPLES OF INDIE JOBS
Administrative Assistant	Administrative Temp
Part-Time Administrative Assistant	Personal Organizer
Computer Programmer	Computer Systems Consultant Owner, Software Design Company
Art Director, Advertising Dept.	Freelance Art Director Owner, Desktop Publishing Company
Human Resources	Freelance Trainer Owner, Human Resources Development Company
Marketing/Communications Executive	Corporate Communications Consultant Owner, Public Relations Firm
Banker	Financial Planner Investment Advisor
Buyer, Retail Stores	Personal Shopper Image Consultant

chapter 3

WHAT IT TAKES TO MAKE IT ON YOUR OWN

We are not here to tell you that self-employment is an easy path. It's not easy to take responsibility for defining your own work, managing your own time and money. As an indie, you'll spend a good portion of your energy drumming up new business. You'll need to risk rejection and uncertainty every time you call someone you don't know and ask for business.

What makes one person more successful than another at self-employment?

Our work with thousands of aspiring indies has shown us that those who succeed at self-employment usually possess a winning combination of *attitudes* and *behaviors* that keep them moving forward and help them succeed. What are the attitudes, behaviors, and skills you need to operate as an independent company? Let's explore the *indie mindset*.

INDIE ATTITUDES

As an indie, your attitude will make you or break you. Here's a quick sketch of some winning thought patterns.

Be Self-Directed

The good thing—and the bad thing—about having a traditional job is that you're directed by outside forces. Your employer provides constant instruction and supervision. Your job is defined, your day is structured, your lifestyle falls into place. Self-employment requires self-direction. You decide what kind of

Working the Phone:
Strategies for Making Business Calls Easier.

1. Before you get on the phone, dress up as if you're going to the office. You'll feel energized and more professional.
2. Try "bookending" your business calls:
   - Call a friend.
   - Describe the actions you plan to take, e.g., "I'm going to make five sales calls."
   - After you complete the task, call the friend again to report your results.
3. Before you make tough business calls, contact a happy client who is glad to hear from you.

work you want to do—and go after it. You must be able to work independently, without supervision. Indies define their own lifestyle, and build their careers around it.

George C. knew he wanted to work from his home. His idea was to launch an information business of some kind. He noticed that his neighborhood was always buzzing with the sound of home improvement efforts. George decided to create a home repair and construction referral service.

First, George did some research at the local library to see if his idea was viable. Then, he wrote a business plan that described how he could make money with his idea. Next, George began interviewing all the local carpenters, landscapers, construction workers, painters, architects, repair people, and interior designers in his community. He found out their prices, called their past customers, and rated each worker on punctuality, quality of craftsmanship, and ability to stick to the estimated budget.

George created an organized, comprehensive referral service listing all the local home repair and construction businesses. He sold his information to homeowners in the form of a catalog that he produced and vended from his house.

George's ability to direct his own efforts made it possible to plan and execute his indie business. George practiced self-direction in several ways:

1. He came up with a unique business idea that excited him and fit his desired lifestyle.
2. He researched his idea to make sure it was viable.
3. He wrote a business plan that showed him and others how he would turn his idea into a profitable business.
4. He took all the steps necessary to create his product (interviewed local workers, established a rating system, printed his catalog).
5. He sold his idea to others.

George's self-direction led to financial rewards and personal satisfaction. With his home repair and construction referral service, George achieved his goal of working from home and running an information business.

Think Positively

Successful indies maintain a very optimistic state of mind. When you're shaping your own career, it becomes all the more important to see events in a positive light. In the ordinary view, a problem is a reason to stop doing something. Successful indies see problems as opportunities for learning. They approach any new situation with confidence.

> **Clara G.**, a self-employed dog walker, spent months passing out fliers and canvassing the neighborhood for potential customers. During her start-up phase, she was dogged by doubts. "I'd wonder if I was fooling myself about my business idea," says Clara. Clara stayed optimistic, however, and eventually her hard work paid off. Within six months, news about Clara's service spread. She soon had more than 25 customers. Within a year, Clara hired additional dog walkers to help her care for her growing canine clientele. Clara reflects, "If I had listened to my negative thoughts during the early days of launching my business, I never would've reached the point where I am today."

As with Clara G., most indies face difficult times when things are not happening as quickly as they would like. During Clara's start-up phase, she could have interpreted her lack of customers from a negative perspective. She could have convinced herself that her dog walking business was a bad idea and quit. Instead, Clara focused on the positive—she knew people needed her service, and that it would take time for her marketing efforts to reach her potential customers.

Believe in Yourself

Self-employment demands self-confidence. Successful indies know that if you believe in yourself, people will believe in you. You can develop self-confidence now by focusing on your past successes, and building on them.

> **Arthur B.** was wondering how he could make some extra money in college. Arthur knew he was good at math. He also seemed adept at helping other people learn: His friends often asked him for assistance with their math homework. He decided to look for work tutoring math students. He made fliers and posted them around the campus.
>
> When the first person called, Arthur was excited but nervous. He wasn't sure if he was really qualified to get paid for tutoring. But then he recalled how many of his friends and family he'd helped with math. Arthur focused on his past successes and began to relax. By the time he met with his first student, Arthur felt confident that he could help this struggling student with his expertise.

> Now that Arthur has ten students he tutors, he can look back at his early experience with relief. "I'm glad I found the confidence to work with that first student. I had the skills. I just needed to believe in myself."

You can increase your self-confidence. Focus on your past successes and use those accomplishments as self-confidence building blocks.

INDIE BEHAVIORS FOR SUCCESS

The right attitudes need to be backed up by action. Here's what successful indies do.

Have Your Own Vision

Successful indies have and hold a personal vision—a mental image of where they want to go and how they want their future lives to be. Vision gives you direction. It tells you where to focus your energies. Once you have a future vision, you can make a plan for reaching that vision.

> **Betsy M.'s** favorite subjects in college were English and art. Although she wasn't sure how she'd do it, Betsy dreamed of creating a children's book that everyone would love to read. Shortly after graduating, Betsy happened to meet a local book publisher at a party. Betsy told him about her idea for a children's book. The publisher asked Betsy to submit some sample drawings to his office. Two weeks later, they met to discuss her book idea further. Over the next four years, Betsy wrote and illustrated three children's books.

Betsy's clear vision allowed her to realize her dream. If she hadn't known that she wanted to write and illustrate children's books, her introduction to a publisher wouldn't have meant much. But because Betsy had a clear picture of her desired success, she was able to cultivate a relationship with this person who played a key role in making her dream become a reality.

Set and Reach Business and Financial Goals

Successful businesses always set business and financial goals. In fact, most companies set goals on a quarterly basis (that is, every three months). Successful indies do the same thing. They set financial goals for the year, and they set short-term goals for each business quarter.

Glen W. knew he wanted to earn $1,000 a month through his lunch delivery service. He sold homemade tuna and chicken salad sandwiches for $5.00 a piece. Glen made $2.50 profit on each sandwich. With a little calculating, Glen figured out that in order to make $1,000 he had to sell 400 sandwiches. When he broke that figure down into four work weeks, Glen determined that he needed to sell 100 sandwiches per week, or 20 sandwiches per day. Glen's financial goal helped him calculate how many sales he should make each day.

By setting a clear financial goal for himself, Glen could estimate the number of sales required to reach his goal ($1,000 = 400 sandwich sales). Glen's financial goal served as a concrete target for success.

Ask for Help

Because indies are self-employed, they have to learn many skills—from sales to bookkeeping to time management to office organization. Successful indies surround themselves with people who have the experience and expertise that they lack. They aren't afraid to ask for help when they don't understand some aspect of their business. They're eager to draw on the wealth of experience and good judgment available to them from people who have already mastered indie skills. Help can come from many sources.

Advisors—Skilled professionals with expertise in specific aspects of running a business. Advisors may include accountants, lawyers, experts in your industry, financial planners, or small-business experts.

Mentors—Your mentor could be an expert in your field, or a mature business person whose career you admire. Mentors may give guidance during the early phases of self-employment. They serve as examples for what you want to become.

Colleagues—Peers who belong to the same profession can offer ideas, resources, and referrals. Colleagues often have experiences and/or information that can help you solve a problem or expand your network. Although some colleagues may be your competitors in business, it's best to cultivate a good relationship with them. Successful indies adopt the attitude that there is enough business for everyone, and colleagues can help each other out.

Be Well Informed

Successful indies take an hour each day to read a trade paper and a national paper. They stay abreast of courses being given in their field. They have subscriptions to any source of information that will add to their knowledge base: cable TV, newsletters, trade publications, online services, and so on.

> It was a Monday morning, and **Jennifer C.** was reading the *Wall Street Journal* as she sipped her first cup of java. She saw an article that grabbed her attention. According to the article, one of her potential clients, Chase Manhattan, was planning to merge with Chemical Bank. Jennifer had an appointment at Chase Manhattan that afternoon to discuss a freelance job as a sales trainer for account managers. Jennifer used the information about Chase's merger to help win the training job. She proposed to improve the account managers' sales skills and help the bank establish its new, expanded identity.

If Jennifer hadn't read the *Wall Street Journal*, she would not have known about the impending merger. She would've gone to her meeting at Chase Manhattan ignorant of a major change in the bank's operations. Because she kept abreast of current events, Jennifer obtained a key piece of information that she incorporated into her sales pitch.

Don't Procrastinate

Successful indies don't procrastinate. They understand that a sense of urgency is necessary for a company to grow. Indies know that if they put things off, they'll get backlogged. If you're busy catching up, you'll miss opportunities for new business. For this reason, successful indies accomplish as much as they can in one day.

> **Carl W.** was tired by 6:30 Monday night, but he still had three more things on his desk to get done. There was a phone call to make, a memo to read, and a set of papers to file. He estimated that all three tasks would take him half an hour to complete. None of the tasks was urgent, but each needed to be completed. He focused his thinking and went to work. He finished everything in 20 minutes, leaving the next day open and clear for new business.

Carl's decision to finish the three tasks before leaving his office freed him from worry about unfinished business. He didn't procrastinate. Like Carl, successful indies don't put off until tomorrow what they can do today.

All of the skills you need to make it as an indie can be learned. You can master each indie attitude and behavior. Begin to develop your indie mindset now, whether you're still in school or working at a traditional job. The sooner you acquire these winning skills, attitudes, and behaviors, the easier it will be to launch your indie career.

Indie Attitudes

Be Self-Directed

Think Positively

Believe In Yourself

Have Your Own Vision

Set and Reach Business and Financial Goals

Ask For Help

Be Well Informed

Don't Procrastinate

GET ORGANIZED NOW

Start practicing the indie mindset with these self-management strategies by Jann Jasper, an organizing consultant and time-management expert in New York City.

1. Aim for effectiveness, not a tidy appearance.

Neatness may be a byproduct of effective work habits, but it's no guarantee. In fact, neatness as an end in itself can be risky: Putting things away just to clear off your desk can cause you to lose or forget them. Remember: Being organized is only a means to an end.

2. Be decisive.

Clutter is rarely caused by insufficient space or time. The culprit is usually indecisiveness. Be selective about what you bring into your office and home. If you know what you value and what your goals are, being decisive and selective is relatively easy.

3. Have a place for everything.

Open your mail in the same place every day, so it doesn't get strewn everywhere. Store all office supplies together to prevent duplicate purchases. Keep magazines you've read separate from those you haven't.

4. Don't use your entire desk surface as a giant in-box.

Instead, determine your next action on every piece of paper and file accordingly. Tasks to be done soon and work in progress go into your hot files. Don't mix hot files with reference files. Keep hot files close at hand in a small file holder designed for the desktop.

Don't follow the false commandment, "Handle each piece of paper only once." But each time you handle a piece of paper, take the next action. That seminar advertisement you've kept on your desk to remind you to decide whether to sign up, the one you've already shuffled ten times today? Take the next action: Either call right now to get the information you need, or make a note in your appointment book to call later.

5. Don't save paper you're not willing to spend time filing.

If you don't file it properly, you'll either forget you have it or you won't be able to find it when you need it. The result is the same as if you'd thrown it out in the first place. Seduced by information, most of us save a great deal of paper we'll never use again. If you can't imagine a specific situation when you'd need to refer to the information again, don't save it.

6. Use your day planner to help clear your desk.

If you fear that out of sight will mean out of mind, jot down a reminder. Day planner formats vary widely. Make sure yours has unstructured space where you can note things to do and jot down ideas for long-term goals.

7. Stop doing the desktop shuffle.

Don't sabotage yourself with constant interruptions. Avoid the bad habit of jumping from one half-finished task to another.

8. Learn to say no.

You will probably die before you have time to do everything you want to do; that's the curse and blessing of being curious and intelligent. The good news is you can choose what to focus on. We have far more freedom than we realize. Very little of what we "have" to do is morally or legally mandatory. Review everything in your life and ask, "What's the worst that can happen if I stop doing this?" Saying no is sometimes the only way you can say yes to what you really value.

9. Beware of stuff.

The more stuff you have, the more stuff you'll have to put away, the more you'll have to clean, and the more to repair or replace eventually. Stop buying things you don't really need just because they're on sale. You can always get more stuff, and you can probably always get more money, but you can never get more time.

10. Do buy more of things you use continually.

Frantic last-minute shopping trips can be averted by purchasing things before your current supply runs out. Whether it's rolls of fax paper or a flattering shirt that goes with everything you own—buy two.

11. Schedule appointments with yourself to get things done.

Appointments aren't just for seeing your dentist. Commit to spending time on the things you keep not getting around to. This works for everything, from taking the next step on that back-burner project to making sure you get your hind end to the gym twice a week.

12. Beware of perfectionism.

Most routine work doesn't need to be done perfectly. Ask yourself: Is my effort disproportionate to the value of the task? Will other, more important projects be delayed as a result? Can I reduce the frequency or level of detail of this task?

section **2**

choosing the **RIGHT BUSINESS**

chapter 4
THE BEST SOURCE OF BUSINESS IDEAS

John C. always gravitated toward three things:

- He enjoyed interviewing people.
- He liked to write.
- He was a current events buff.

As a kid in grammar school, John wrote amusing tales about the people in his neighborhood. Editor of his high school yearbook, he also wrote articles for the school newspaper. In college, John studied journalism and international affairs. During his summer vacation, he worked as an intern for the town newspaper.

John graduated from college aiming for a career as a freelance journalist. He liked the lifestyle because he could work independently, from home, setting his own hours. He also liked the fact that, as a freelancer, he could write for and be paid by several publications at the same time. John researched the various publications in his area. He submitted articles to every local newspaper, magazine, and newsletter that featured in-depth coverage of current events.

John landed his first assignment with a consumer newsletter. He was paid to review consumer products as they came out on the market. Over time, John built a name for himself as a consumer information expert. He picked up writing assignments from consumer magazines and national newspapers. He wrote a syndicated column for regional newspapers. He even obtained a weekly 3-minute segment on a radio news program.

After ten years of freelance writing, John switched gears and launched his own company. Using the contacts and skills from his previous work, John created a consumer information hotline and news service. He hired other reporters to investigate and rate new commercial products as they came onto the market. Within two years, John's company became the resource for evaluating the safety and value of consumer goods.

You don't wear a business like a coat. Your business venture has to come from inside you.

John's story illustrates how to pursue an indie career from the inside out. For John, writing, interviewing people, and keeping track of current events were things he always enjoyed and did effortlessly. His indie businesses, freelance writing, and his own consumer information news service, emerged directly from his core talents, skills, and interests. Successful indies find their business ideas in a similar way. They don't just latch onto a business idea and wear it like a coat. Rather, they pull their business ideas from inside themselves. They figure out the right business for them based on who they are and what they do best.

Satisfying indie careers combine

- Natural talents
- Learned skills
- Personal interests
- Lifestyle preferences
- Current business trends

John C. identified his *talents* (writing, interviewing people, *interests* (current events, gathering information), and *skills* (in-depth reporting on current events) while he was in school. After graduation, he pursued the *lifestyle* of a freelance writer. John also identified a *trend*, consumer education, that he could write about. Satisfying self-employment begins with some degree of self-assessment and self-knowledge. Before you can determine the work you should do, you need to decipher the kind of person you are.

In the next five chapters we're going to do just that. We're going to explore your talents, your learned skills, your personal interests, and your lifestyle preferences. We're also going to show you how to identify and use current business trends to build your indie business. We're going to help you uncover who you are so that you can follow an indie career path that fits you.

You'll be answering a lot of questions and examining yourself from many angles. After you do these exercises, you'll be able to put the information together and determine the right indie business ideas for *you*.

Before we begin these self-assessment exercises, we want to warn you against the three major misconceptions that stop individuals from choosing the right business.

Common Mistakes

- Denying who you are and opting for stability
- Making money your only career goal
- Assuming that below-average grades in school means you'll flunk in business

Denying Who You Are And Opting For Stability

From childhood on, **Jeanette P.** had entrepreneurial dreams. She wanted to open her own company to create a line of beautiful, innovative clothing for full-figured women. Jeanette was bigger than her peers, and she always noticed the lack of fashionable clothes for people her size.

In grade school art classes, Jeanette drew and painted the ensembles she imagined. In junior high school, Jeanette learned how to use a sewing machine. By the time she entered high school, Jeanette was making her own clothes. She got a lot of positive feedback for her designs. Often friends liked Jeanette's clothes so much, they asked her to make the same items for them.

When Jeanette told her parents that she wanted to start he own clothing design business, they were very discouraging. "There's no stability in that kind of work," they said. "You need to find a real job." No one in Jeanette's family was self-employed, and they did not have the indie mindset. Despite her family's lack of enthusiasm for her business idea, Jeanette quietly kept her dream alive.

As high school graduation approached, Jeanette's parents insisted that she go to a liberal arts college for a teaching degree. They believed that a teaching career would ensure financial stability and job security for their daughter. Jeanette lacked the confidence to tell her parents what she really wanted—to take courses in fashion design and small-business management. Dutifully, she packed herself off to a liberal arts college.

Jeanette forgot her dream while she pursued a teaching degree. She specialized in art and English education. After graduation, she became a third-grade teacher in a local public school. Jeanette enjoyed teaching at first, but after a couple of years, she became increasingly disillusioned. Jeanette wondered what was wrong with her. The students were stimulating, teaching was challenging, but *something was missing.*

Ultimately, denying your true talents, interests, and skills leads to career dissatisfaction.

"Something is missing" is a common refrain from people who follow a career path that doesn't fit them. Jeanette's story is an important one; she represents the many people who know what they want to do but fear taking the risk. Instead of pursuing her indie dream, Jeanette took the safe route. She got that teaching degree. She went for stability.

Jeanette did have a job, but she didn't have job satisfaction. She put her true desire to start a fashion design business on hold.

Making Money Your Only Career Goal

Paul was the kind of guy who always knew where a party was. And if there wasn't a party, he'd start one. Paul was voted most popular guy in his high school senior class, and elected president of his graduating class in college. Paul seemed to be a natural public relations expert. But Paul couldn't imagine a career in that field. He'd grown up in an affluent family and felt pressure to make a lot of money.

Paul majored in economics in college, taking the subjects that really interested him—English, psychology, sociology—as electives. As Paul headed toward graduation, he knew that a job in the financial sector was the career path expected of him. Investment banking seemed like a perfect fit. His affluent classmates could become his clients. He could make a lot of money and everyone would be impressed.

Five years down the road, Paul was frustrated. Yes, he was making the kind of money expected of him. Yes, he enjoyed the luxury of having a car service transport him to work. Yes, he dined with the rich and famous. And, yes his clients were very satisfied with his performance. In fact, Paul was very good at targeting and investing in extremely lucrative funds. But something inside Paul was dying.

Paul's days started at 6 A.M. and were booked with meetings, luncheons, dinners, and paperwork. It was not unusual for Paul to work until 11 at night. Because his business day was so long, Paul had very little time to socialize or network with his friends—things he enjoyed doing most. When he did have free time, Paul usually slept. How could he be so successful financially, and feel so empty inside?

While money is an important consideration in any career path, making money the sole factor in your career choice usually leads to unhappiness. Paul chose his career path based on one need: making a lot of money. He accomplished his goal, but he ignored his primary talents and interests—socializing, networking, connecting, planning events.

Real success involves combining your financial goals with your talents, skills, interests, and values.

Like Paul, you may be tempted to use money as the only consideration when you launch your indie career. We advise against it. We encourage you to use the exercises in this book to combine your financial goals with your talents, skills, interests and values. Trust us: You'll feel better about the work you do. You'll be a happier person.

Assuming That Below Average Grades In School Mean You Won't Succeed In Business

Karen K. got below-average grades. She had a learning disability and worked extremely hard just to pass her courses. Karen compared herself to her classmates, and assumed she wasn't very smart. She didn't know she had a kind of intelligence that wasn't evident in school.

In high school, Karen did not have many positive experiences. She didn't feel smart enough to join any of the clubs. Not particularly athletic, she didn't get involved with sports. Karen had a large circle of friends, and she was able to have fun outside of school. But in school, Karen's mediocre academic performance chipped away at her confidence. By the time she graduated from high school, Karen expected very little of herself.

At her parents' insistence, Karen went to college. She had a hard time deciding on a major. She enjoyed certain courses like sociology and philosophy. But the truth was that Karen's heart was not in school. She wanted out.

Karen's lack of success at the game of school made her eager to try her hand at business. During summer vacations, she took part-time jobs in retail stores. It was at these jobs that Karen had her first experience of excelling among her peers. In selling, Karen needed skills that weren't taught at school. These skills included relating to a wide range of people, making conversation, building rapport, asking good questions, and getting the business. These abilities came naturally to Karen.

> At her sales jobs, Karen was consistently number one. Each week she consistently sold more products that any of the other salespeople. Karen made hundreds of dollars in commissions, and invariably became the most valued salesperson. Finally, Karen's talents and interests could shine.

Karen's story clearly illustrates the fact that poor grades in school don't indicate how you'll do in the business world. The skills it took for her to excel at sales—social skills and business savvy—had nothing to do with academics or grade point averages. She cultivated these abilities outside school.

Many students make the incorrect assumption that their grade point averages will make or break their business careers. Our experience with aspiring indies shows that the opposite may be true. Successful indies are often underachievers in school, but overachievers in the world of business. Their talents and abilities often flourish outside of formal classroom settings.

HIGH GEAR OR LOW GEAR?

Our experience with aspiring indies reveals two distinct "energy profiles." Each has advantages and disadvantages. Read each of the following statements and circle the response (a or b) that best fits your personality. Then read the tips that follow.

1. **When someone asks me to try something new, my immediate response is usually**
   (a) "yes"
   (b) "no"

2. **When faced with an unpleasant task, I normally**
   (a) push ahead and complete it
   (b) set it aside and find something else to do

3. **In school, my teachers described me as**
   (a) a conscientious student who completed his/her assignments
   (b) a bright student who did not apply him-/herself fully

4. **I was the kind of student who**
   (a) worked hard in all of my classes
   (b) worked hard only in the classes that interested me

5. I am the kind of person who
   (a) tackles problems quickly by taking immediate action
   (b) ignores problems until they require immediate action

6. When someone criticizes my work, I usually
   (a) assume the criticism is valid, and work harder next time
   (b) feel offended and decide to stop trying

7. I like my days to be
   (a) fully booked with many activities
   (b) loosely planned with lots of options

8. In my relationships, I normally
   (a) jump in and see what I can offer the other person
   (b) step back and see what the other person has to offer me

9. When it comes to deadlines
   (a) I usually meet them
   (b) I usually extend them

10. When I have an idea
   (a) I usually take action on it immediately
   (b) I usually think about it a lot, but rarely take action

11. In general, I am known as
   (a) a rule keeper
   (b) a rule breaker

12. When I am not sure what to do next
   (a) I whip out my To Do list and tackle the next item.
   (b) I watch TV, or find some other forms of distraction

Tally the As and Bs: As: ____ Bs _______

If you checked off more As than Bs, you have a high-gear personality. If you have more Bs than As, you're in low gear. One gear is not superior to the other: Each has its own pitfalls and benefits. Find your energy profile below, and see how it might affect your work habits.

High-Gear Profile

If you checked off more As than Bs, you are probably:

Extremely hardworking.

A natural leader and organizer.

Super responsible.

Self-reliant.

Conscientious.

Someone who seeks praise and approval.

An initiator and risk taker.

Someone with strong powers of concentration.

A time optimist (an overextender).

Plusses

You're willing and able to do groundwork for maintaining your own ventures.

You're able to take on challenging projects and complete them.

You're responsible to the needs of customers and staff.

You gain trust and respect through work.

You're determined to learn from your mistakes.

Possible Pitfalls

You tend to drive yourself to exhaustion.

You're often plagued by the feeling you haven't done enough.

You don't know when to quit or say no.

You may get caught in work that's not rewarding financially or personally.

Self-Management Tips

Build breaks into your day, and take at least one day off per week.

Set aside time for reflecting on the Big Picture of your business.

Keep track of your hours and bill accordingly.

Focus on thinking smarter, not working harder.

Low-Gear Profile

If you checked off more Bs than As, you're probably:

Naturally bright.

Exceptionally talented.

Someone who makes others responsible.

Someone who works hard when you're interested.

Someone who avoids things that don't interest you.

Highly idealistic.

An original thinker.

Risk averse.

A time waster.

Plusses

You have a wealth of natural ability that can be applied to business.

You're able to solve problems creatively.

You have a talent for persuading others to see your viewpoint.

You produce excellent work when you apply yourself.

You are comfortable going against the tide, launching new ideas.

Possible Pitfalls

You often lack self-discipline and fail to follow through on ideas.

You tend to take rejection personally and quit.

You have trouble owning your mistakes and learning from them.

You set expectations too high, and are easily disappointed.

You often spend more time putting off work than doing it.

Self-Management Tips

Create a daily schedule, and stick to it.

Do "dirty tasks" first, and reward yourself for completing them.

Break big ideas down into concrete goals; take daily steps to reach your goals.

Learn how to depersonalize rejection.

Join a support group for support and accountability.

Now that you know the common pitfalls to avoid, you can go on to uncover the best indie business idea for you. Good luck. Be honest, and prepare to be surprised.

chapter 5
SCOUTING YOUR TALENTS

Herb B. was a very industrious child. From the moment he could walk, he was busy taking things apart. At age three, Herb took apart his bedroom doorknobs. At age five, he removed the kitchen cabinet doors. By the time he was eight, Herb had succeeded in dismantling the toaster and the TV.

Herb also loved to build electronic devices and communicate through them. In his teens, he designed and built his own ham radio. At night, he conducted conversations with people all over the world.

Today, Herb is an electrical engineer. He owns a business designing and installing home security systems. Herb took three of his natural talents—taking things apart, building electronic devices, communicating with people—and incorporated them into his indie business.

Everyone has natural talents. But many people take their natural talents—the abilities and aptitudes they were born with—for granted. They mistakenly think, "If it's easy for me to do, it's no big deal."

People are happiest when they use the talents they were born with to make money and build a career. Successful indies like Herb B. understand this fact, and take their natural talents seriously.

As an indie, you'll want to become familiar with your natural talents. The better you know them, the easier it will be for you to incorporate them into your business idea. Then your business will be a natural extension of yourself.

What are your natural talents? It's critical to identify these abilities of yours and make them part of your indie venture. If you aren't sure what your innate abilities are, ask the people who know you best for some ideas. Approach close friends and family members. Ask your favorite teachers. Let them tell you what natural talents they see in you. The following checklist will also help.

TALLYING YOUR TALENTS

Read the following checklists. Put a check next to any ability you possess. Use the blank lines to write down any talents you have that aren't on the lists.

Interpersonal Talents

__ I can work with others.
__ I can work alone.
__ I can empathize with people.
__ I can attend to other people's needs.
__ I can cooperate, be a team player.
__ I can entertain people.
__ I can express ideas.
__ I can handle emotional crises.
__ I can help others.
__ I can lead people.
__ I can listen attentively.
__ I can make people laugh.
__ I can manage people.
__ I can mediate, resolve conflict.
__ I can motivate people.
__ I can perform for an audience.
__ I can persuade people.
__ I can relate to a wide range of people.
__ I can remain calm under pressure.
__ I can show warmth and support.
__ I can teach people.
__ ____________________
__ ____________________

Creative Talents

__ I'm good at expressing myself verbally.
__ I'm good at learning languages.
__ I'm a good actor.
__ I can cook.
__ I can dance.
__ I can draw.
__ I can sing.
__ I'm good at seeing light and shadow.
__ I have good color perception.
__ I have good spatial perception.
__ I have a good memory for design.
__ I have good recall for objects.
__ I have good pitch discrimination.
__ I can remember rhythms.
__ I have a sense of composition.
__ I have a sense of proportion.
__ I have a sense of style.
__ I have a sense of texture.
__ I have a good memory for shape.
__ I have a good memory for sound.
__ I have good taste discrimination.
__ I have good tone discrimination.
__ I have a good memory for words.
__ ____________________
__ ____________________

Physical Talents

__ I have speed.
__ I have stamina.
__ I have balance.
__ I have good physical coordination.
__ I have hand-eye coordination.
__ I have flexibility.
__ I have powers of concentration.
__ I have strength.
__ I have manual dexterity.
__ ______________________
__ ______________________

Mechanical Talents

__ I like assembling things.
__ I like taking things apart.
__ I like maintaining equipment.
__ I like repairing things.
__ I like using hand tools.
__ I like working with machines.
__ I like diagnosing mechanical problems.
__ I like constructing things.
__ I like operating equipment.
__ ______________________
__ ______________________

Ecology/Nature Talents

__ I can endure the elements (heat, cold, wind, rain, snow).
__ I'm good with animals.
__ I'm good with plants.
__ I am resourceful and comfortable outdoors.
__ I like to grow things.
__ I like to garden.
__ I can survive in the wilderness.
__ I like to take care of living things.
__ I like to work with nature.
__ ______________________
__ ______________________

Organizational Talents

__ I can perform many tasks at once.
__ I can analyze needs.
__ I can attend to details.
__ I can break things down into smaller units.
__ I can create order out of disorder.
__ I can find and correct mistakes.
__ I can gather information and data.
__ I can keep records.
__ I can organize people.
__ I can prioritize.
__ I can plan projects.
__ I can see steps to achieving goals.
__ I can set up systems for getting things done.
__ I can sort and categorize things.
__ ______________________
__ ______________________

Mental/Intellectual Talents

__ I'm good at analyzing facts and ideas.
__ I'm good at analyzing and solve problems.
__ I'm good at forecasting trends.
__ I'm good at generating and developing ideas.
__ I'm good at inventing things.

__ I'm good at making decisions.
__ I'm good at perceiving/defining cause-and-effect relationships.
__ I'm good at retaining information.
__ I'm good at thinking logically.
__ I'm good at using statistics.
__ I'm good at working with abstract material and concepts.
__ ______________________________
__ ______________________________

From the talent checklists, select the five talents that you would most like to include in your indie work life. Write them in order of enjoyment. (You can combine talents on a line if you feel they're related.)

Top-Five Natural Talents

1. ______________________________

2. ______________________________

3. ______________________________

4. ______________________________

5. ______________________________

It's important to remember that natural business talents often reveal themselves indirectly. Were you the class clown? You may be a natural salesperson in disguise.

INDIE TALENT PROFILES

To illustrate how natural talents transfer into indie careers, we've mapped out the talents of successful indies in a variety of industries and professions. Read the following "talent profiles" and see if any of these businesses or professions fits you.

Indie: Karen DeMauro
Profession: Actor
Indie Path: Acting since the age of six. Majored in theater in college. After graduation, taught for eight years. Went indie creating her own company as an artist-in-residence around the United States. Wrote original musicals for public schools; survived mostly on income from grants. After several years, turned this business into a multiservice company, The Acting Center.

Where Is She Now?
The Acting Center has expanded its offerings to include coaching for Broadway actors, professional storytelling, live solo performing, and corporate presentation skills training.

Karen's Top Talents

Powers of concentration
Physical stamina
Ability to entertain people
Ability to empathize
Word memory

Indie: John Follis
Profession: Advertising Creative Director
Indie Path: Showed artistic talent in college. Advised in junior year of college to transfer to school with better art department. Majored in advertising design. After college, worked full time in corporate environment as junior-level art director. Got fired from a few companies. Left a few companies. After getting fired for the third time, picked up a freelance assignment through networking. Took one more full-time job. When that ended, decided to open a freelance business. Worked with ad agencies on a project basis. Gradually built a client base. Formed a partnership with an excellent sales person.

Where Is He Now?
Flying solo since the partnership broke up after a few years. Running his own corporation—Follis Advertising, Inc., New York City.

John's Top Talents

Forecasting trends
Generating and developing ideas
Expressing ideas
Verbal ability
Powers of persuasion

Indie: Belinda Clarke
Profession: Caterer
Indie Path: Went to restaurant management program in South Africa, where she worked part time as a restaurant worker and part time as restaurant manager. She went to Sussex, England and trained in a hotel kitchen for eight months.

Where Is She Now?
Running her own New York City–based catering company. Her first client was the South African ambassador to the United Nations.

Belinda's Top Talents

Ability to cook
Physical stamina
Sense of composition
Setting up systems for getting things done
Managing people

Indie: Julia Kosolapova
Profession: Computer Programmer
Indie Path: Landed a full-time job with a financial company while still in college. Garnered a master's degree in economics.

Where Is She Now?
Currently working at another financial company in a full-time indie job.

Julia's Top Talents

Logical thinking
Analyzing facts and ideas

Breaking things down into smaller units
Seeing steps to achieving goals
Analyzing and solving problems

Indie: Robert Gould
Profession: Computer Technician
Indie Path: After high school, worked as draftsman for an architectural firm. Went on to become a general contractor who built home additions. At night and on weekends, worked in theaters as an electrical technician. Eventually invited to work on Broadway as an electrical technician. While there, wrote a book on a compendium of theater specifications designed into a database.

Where Is He Now?
Robert's database project got him into working on computers as an indie.

Robert's Top Talents
Assembling things and taking things apart
Diagnosing mechanical problems
Using hand tools
Operating equipment
Analyzing and solving problems

Indie: Neville Bean
Profession: Fashion Designer
Indie Path: Learned to sew in high school. Made and sold prom dresses and other outfits to friends. In college, sold one-of-a-kind clothing to boutiques. After college, got several design jobs in small companies. Started and ran freelance design business for three years. Took two more full-time jobs to build business skills. Relaunched indie fashion design studio.

Where Is She Now?
Owner of Neville Bean Designs, a full-range trends and forecasting design studio.

Neville's Top Talents
Forecast trends
Attend to details
Assemble things

Sense of style and composition
Color perception and sense of texture

Indie: Alice Simpson
Profession: Graphic Designer
Indie Path: Started out as fashion illustrator. Worked as art director in small agencies and design studios using illustration and graphic design skills. Realized she could make more money as a freelancer. Worked from home as a graphic designer for various companies.

Where Is She Now?
Alice has recently moved into product development and licensing of her illustrations.

Alice's Top Talents
Ability to work alone
Ability to generate and develop ideas
Spatial perception
Sense of composition
Ability to analyze and solve problems

Indie: Susan Steiger
Profession: Lawyer
Indie Path: During third year of law school, interned at a law firm. Graduated at top of class, and took a full-time job in a different prestigious law firm for two years. Held another full time job in an entertainment law firm for two years. Went out on her own for two years. Held a full-time job for eight years.

Where Is She Now?
Returned to self-employment again as an expert in entertainment law.

Susan's Top Talents
Logical thinking
Gathering information and data
Retaining information
Mediating, resolving conflict
Ability with words

Indie: Bernadette Kathryn
Profession: Personal trainer and massage therapist
Indie Path: Taught exercise classes while in high school. Turned that into a full-time job. Went into corporate training. Met someone who wanted to finance and open an exercise facility. Owned and ran exercise studio for five years. Services offered included corporate training, private training, and exercise classes. Closed business and did private training exclusively while going back to school to learn massage.

Where Is She Now?
Still building her private client base. Now combines massage and personal training.

Bernadette's Top Talents

Good physical coordination
Stamina
Ability to listen attentively
Analyzing and solving problems
Motivating and teaching people
Helping others

Indie: Agnes Lee
Profession: Psychotherapist
Indie Path: Obtained master's degree in social work. Focused on clinical social work, with an emphasis in developmental psychology. Worked for four years at a social service agency, counseling children and adolescents. Took courses at night to build skills in family and marriage counseling. Got certificate in family counseling from institute. Opened part-time private practice while still holding full-time job. Established specialty in marriage and family counseling.

Where Is She Now?
Eventually left job and built full-time practice.

Agnes' Top Talents:

Empathy
Helping others
Perceiving and defining cause-and-effect relationships
Listening attentively
Handling emotional crises

Indie: Blair Wijnkoop
Profession: Restaurateur
Indie Path: Hated high school. Transferred to a community college that gave both high school and college credits. Transferred to a state university, then to U.C.L.A. Graduated with a bachelor's degree in marketing. Throughout college, worked in restaurants. Went from working as dishwasher to busboy to waiter. Moved to New York City; pursued work in advertising agencies. Got a restaurant job to pay the bills. Realized that waiting tables paid better than ad agency jobs. Was eventually hired by small business owner to work for destination management corporation (setting up travel programs for corporate employees). A friend at this company became partner in first indie venture. Leased a warehouse on the waterfront overlooking the Statue of Liberty. Spent a sleep-deprived year renting this waterfront space out for parties. Made an excellent profit. Invested some money into a restaurant in South Beach, Florida. Invested in another restaurant in Manhattan, Flamingo East.

Where Is He Now?
Became involved with operating and managing Flamingo East. Has been there ever since.

Blair's Top Talents:

Attending to other people's needs
Physical stamina
Setting up systems for getting things done
Attending to details
Ability to perform many tasks at once

Indie: Robin Kormos
Profession: Video Producer
Indie Path: A born indie. After completing her formal education, learned typography and photography for graphics. Started finding people who were making their own films and videos. Volunteered on other people's films for two years just to be close to film and video equipment. Once plugged into the film producing network, started getting paying jobs. Saw that she could use graphic arts skills to make money. Called animators and learned how to do graphics for film credits and subtitles. Started doing graphics for eight animation houses. Found this work lucrative but unfulfilling. Made her own art films that got distributed internationally but didn't make much money. While doing titles for films, started selecting a particular kind of client—organizations that were contributing to mankind. Through own environmental video, got international distribution. Hooked up with business partner who shares her ideology.

Where Is She Now?

Still producing videos for organizations that are doing good works. Doing her own projects, such as a children's television series for worldwide television on the side. This time hitting big markets for wider commercial distribution.

Robin's Top Talents:

Remaining calm under pressure
Generating and developing ideas
Spatial perception
Sense of timing and composition
Planning projects
Attending to details

chapter 6
DEFINING YOUR SKILL BANK

Zelda K.'s hobby was baking. Her mother was an excellent cook, and spent many hours passing her skills on to Zelda. By the time Zelda was in high school, she'd created several of her own recipes for cookies, brownies, cakes, and candy. With her parents' encouragement, Zelda decided to pursue baking as a profession. Her dream was to open her own bakery featuring "designer desserts."

Before that could happen, however, Zelda needed to build up her skills. She enrolled in a culinary school, and studied important subjects such as food preparation, food presentation, nutrition, basic marketing, and cooking techniques. By the time Zelda graduated, she possessed enough knowledge and training to call herself a full-fledged professional baker.

Your skill bank is full of skills you've learned through the years. Like Zelda, we obtain many of our skills in school. You learned reading, writing, English, history, science, and math in an academic setting. Learned skills are also transferred in less formal settings. Perhaps you learned to play tennis at camp. You might have learned to file at your first part-time office job. You may have learned how to sew or do carpentry through someone's personal instruction.

Learned skills differ from natural talents. First, they're acquired; you aren't just born with them. Second, you can build upon them. For example, once you learn how to write, you can go on to learn how to write screenplays. You can keep adding to your learned skill base throughout life. A fireman can go back to school and learn accounting. A teacher can acquire skills in graphic design.

You'll need to understand what your skills are and keep building on them. To get started, try enumerating all the skills you currently possess and any skills you want to develop. Once you come up with a full list, you can go through them and decide which skills you'd like to incorporate into your work life. The following is a list of skills covering a wide range of areas. First, check the skills you've learned and can use reasonably well. Next, check the skills you want to develop. Use the blank lines at the end of the exercise to add any skills you have that aren't included on the list.

YOUR SKILL BANK

Know	Want to develop	
____	____	abnormal psychology
____	____	accounting
____	____	acting techniques
____	____	advertising writing
____	____	aeronautics
____	____	anatomy
____	____	animal care
____	____	animal grooming
____	____	art direction
____	____	auto mechanics
____	____	baby-sitting
____	____	basketball
____	____	baseball
____	____	beading
____	____	biology
____	____	bookkeeping
____	____	building design
____	____	business telephone skills
____	____	business writing
____	____	calligraphy
____	____	camera operation
____	____	cardiopulmonary resuscitation (CPR)
____	____	carpentry
____	____	chemistry

"The most critical skill is acting techniques. If you don't have craft, you are at the mercy of your own emotions and the whims of the audience."

Karen DeMauro, Professional Actress and Storyteller

Know	Want to develop	
____	____	civil engineering
____	____	clinical psychology
____	____	chess
____	____	clothing design
____	____	computer languages
____	____	computer maintenance
____	____	computer networking
____	____	computer operating systems
____	____	computer programming
____	____	computer repair
____	____	computer science
____	____	computer software design
____	____	computer wiring
____	____	creative writing
____	____	construction

"Computer maintenance and repair is a must."

Robert Gould, Computer Technician

____	____	cooking techniques
____	____	curriculum development
____	____	dancing
____	____	debating
____	____	desktop publishing
____	____	dog training
____	____	drafting
____	____	drawing
____	____	driving
____	____	dubbing
____	____	economics
____	____	editing

"Learn from the people who are leaders in their fields. Learn from the best. Expose yourself to and seek wisdom from the people you consider the best at what they do. Seek those people out."

John Follis, Advertising Creative Director

Know	Want to develop	
____	____	electrical engineering
____	____	electrical wiring
____	____	embroidery
____	____	farming
____	____	filing, alphabetical
____	____	filing, numerical
____	____	film camera operation
____	____	film developing
____	____	film editing
____	____	film production
____	____	first aid
____	____	fitness training
____	____	food preparation
____	____	food presentation
____	____	foreign language
____	____	furniture design
____	____	gardening
____	____	geography
____	____	geology
____	____	grant writing

"Learning business skills changed my life. I would still be working on projects for no money if I hadn't developed strong business skills."

Robin Kormos, Video Producer

Know	Want to develop	
____	____	graphic design
____	____	gymnastics
____	____	hairstyling
____	____	history
____	____	ice skating
____	____	illustration
____	____	interior design
____	____	interviewing skills
____	____	investment banking
____	____	jewelry design
____	____	jewelry construction
____	____	journalistic writing
____	____	juggling
____	____	kinesthesiology
____	____	knitting
____	____	landscape design
____	____	landscape maintenance
____	____	language skills
____	____	law
____	____	leather work
____	____	legal systems
____	____	legal writing
____	____	linguistics
____	____	litigation
____	____	lighting
____	____	machine design
____	____	machine maintenance
____	____	machine operation
____	____	makeup artistry
____	____	management
____	____	marketing

"The most essential skill is managing people."

Blair Wijnkoop, Restaurateur

Know	Want to develop	
____	____	martial arts
____	____	masonry
____	____	mathematics
____	____	mechanical engineering
____	____	merchandising
____	____	money management
____	____	movement techniques
____	____	music appreciation
____	____	music composition
____	____	music reading
____	____	navigation
____	____	needlepoint
____	____	negotiation
____	____	nutrition
____	____	office systems
____	____	organizational development

"The two most important learned skills are legal writing and negotiation. You can't be a good negotiator if you don't know what your position is. Writing becomes critical." Susan Steiger, Lawyer

____	____	ornithology
____	____	painting
____	____	patient care
____	____	pattern making
____	____	personality theory
____	____	photography

Know	Want to develop	
____	____	physics
____	____	physiology
____	____	play musical instrument
____	____	plumbing
____	____	political science
____	____	pottery

"To be effective in fashion design, technical skills like pattern making and sewing are really crucial. Knowing how clothes are constructed allows me to design a complete project that's ready to go into production." Neville Bean, Fashion Designer

____	____	psychological development
____	____	psychological assessment
____	____	psychological pathology
____	____	public policy
____	____	public speaking
____	____	purchasing
____	____	reading to the blind
____	____	research
____	____	religious studies
____	____	restoring furniture
____	____	restoring paintings
____	____	sailing

"To be effective as a psychotherapist, you need to be able to hear someone's story and make an assessment. Psychological assessment is a critical skill for anyone in the mental health field."

Agnes Lee, Psychotherapist

Know	**Want to develop**	
____	____	screenwriting
____	____	sculpting
____	____	selling
____	____	sewing
____	____	sign language
____	____	skating
____	____	skiing
____	____	soccer
____	____	sociology
____	____	sound engineering
____	____	swimming
____	____	teaching
____	____	tennis
____	____	theories of psychological intervention
____	____	time management
____	____	trading stocks and bonds
____	____	typing
____	____	typography
____	____	video production
____	____	voice (singing)
____	____	voice (speaking)
____	____	weaving
____	____	welding
____	____	woodworking
____	____	word processing

"The most important skill is definitely time management. Everything else can be purchased, but only you can manage your time."

Belinda Clarke, Caterer and Personal Chef

Know	**Want to develop**	
____	____	____________________
____	____	____________________
____	____	____________________
____	____	____________________
____	____	____________________
____	____	____________________
____	____	____________________
____	____	____________________
____	____	____________________

Now, look at all of the skills you've checked off as skills you know. Select the top five you'd most like to include in your work life. (You can include more than one skill on a line if you feel they are related.)

Skills I Have and Want To Use At Work

1. ______________________________

2. ______________________________

3. ______________________________

4. ______________________________

5. ______________________________

Next, look at all of the skills you want to develop. Select the top five you'd most like to include in your work life.

Skills I Want To Develop and Use At Work

1. ______________________________

2. ______________________________

3. ______________________________

4. ______________________________

5. ______________________________

You've just completed an indie skills inventory. We'll be using your top five learned skills and the top five skills you want to develop to help you come up with your indie business idea. For now, give yourself credit for a job well done.

The next chapter will focus on clarifying your interests. Before you turn to those assessment exercises, read the skill profiles of the indie professionals we first sited in the last chapter. You can see how other people have successfully combined their talents and skills in their indie ventures.

Profession:	Actor		
Talents:	Powers of concentration	**Skills:**	Acting techniques
	Physical stamina		Dance
	Entertain people		Movement techniques
	Ability to empathize		Public speaking
	Word memory		Voice, singing, and speaking

Profession:	Advertising Consultant		
Talents:	Identify trends	**Skills:**	Advertising writing
	Generate and develop ideas		Art direction
	Express ideas		Marketing
	Ability with words		Psychological development
	Persuade people		Typography

Profession:	Caterer		
Talents:	Ability to cook	**Skills:**	Cooking techniques
	Physical stamina		Food preparation
	Sense of composition		Food presentation
	Set up systems for getting things done		Nutrition
	Manage people		Time management

Profession:	Computer Programmer		
Talents:	Think logically	**Skills:**	Computer science
	Analyze facts and ideas		Computer languages
	Break things down into smaller units		Computer operating systems
	See steps to achieving goals		Computer programming
	Analyze and solve problems		Mathematics

Profession:	Computer Technician		
Talents:	Assemble things/take things apart	**Skills:**	Computer science
	Diagnose mechanical problems		Computer wiring and networking
	Use hand tools		Machine maintenance & repair
	Operate equipment		Electrical wiring
	Analyze and solve problems		Computer operation systems
Profession:	Fashion Designer		
Talents:	Forecast trends	**Skills:**	Merchandising
	Attend to details		Pattern making
	Assemble things		Sewing
	Sense of style & composition		Illustration
	Color perception & sense of texture		Clothing design
Profession:	Graphic Designer		
Talents:	Ability to work alone	**Skills:**	Typography
	Generating/developing ideas		Graphic design
	Spatial perception		Art direction
	Sense of composition		Drawing
	Analyzing/solving problems		Desktop publishing
Profession:	Lawyer		
Talents:	Think logically	**Skills:**	Law
	Gather information & data		Legal writing
	Retain information		Legal systems
	Mediate, resolve conflict		Negotiation
	Ability with words		Public speaking
Profession:	Personal Trainer		
Talents:	Good physical coordination & stamina	**Skills:**	Anatomy
	Listening attentively		Physiology
	Analyzing/solving problems		First aid and CPR
	Motivating/teaching people		Kinesthesiology
	Helping others		Fitness training

Profession: Psychotherapist

Talents:
- Empathy
- Helping others
- Perceiving/defining cause and effect relationships
- Listening attentively
- Handling emotional crises

Skills:
- Abnormal psychology
- Psychological development
- Clinical psychology
- Psychological assessment
- Theories of psychiatric intervention

Profession: Restaurateur

Talents:
- Attend to other people's needs
- Physical stamina
- Set up systems for getting things done
- Attend to details
- Ability to multitask

Skills:
- Accounting
- Management
- Marketing
- Purchasing
- Food preparation

Profession: Video Producer

Talents:
- Remain calm under pressure
- Generating and developing ideas
- Spatial perception
- Sense of timing & composition
- Planning projects & attend to details

Skills:
- Film and video production
- Film and video editing
- Directing
- Management
- Business writing

---

chapter 7
PINPOINTING YOUR PASSIONS

Even in high school, **Holly K.** knew that she liked everything related to decorating, design, and style. She spent hours decorating her room. She enjoyed dressing her friends. She pored over art and fashion magazines. Holly couldn't enter a room without noticing the colors, shapes, and textures to be found there, and mentally redecorating the space.

Holly applied to the nearest design institute for college. She wasn't sure what she wanted to focus on academically. She considered majoring in either interior decorating or fashion design, but she wasn't sure if the course work for either of those majors would really interest her. Holly researched the course requirements for each major. When Holly saw the technical skills involved in fashion design (sewing, pattern making), she knew it wasn't for her. Similarly, when she realized that interior decorating involved subjects like drafting, floor plans, and art history, she lost her enthusiasm.

With a little more research, Holly eventually found a major that did interest her: package design, the study of how to package products so that people would buy them. Package design encompassed all of Holly's interests in design, style, and decorating. It also involved a wide range of subjects, most of which really interested her: marketing, advertising, writing, product packaging, and graphic design.

After graduating, Holly became an indie graphic designer and packaging consultant. She now designs logos, packaging, and advertisements for home furnishing companies and clothing manufacturers.

An *interest* is any subject area that catches your attention and gives you energy. Interests spark our curiosity. A strong interest motivates us to learn. Smart indies make sure that their business ideas incorporate at least some of their strong interests. This is how they make sure their work remains stimulating and energizing for a long period of time.

In the example above, Holly exhibited three consistent strong interests during high school—she liked design, decorating, and style. Holly enjoyed her studies in package design because it combined topics that caught her attention and stirred her enthusiasm.

Interests have an evolutionary quality. They grow and change over time. A student may start out with an interest in architecture that develops into an interest in three-dimensional design, which develops further into an interest in furniture design. Interests usually begin with a broad topic. As you study the broad topic, specific aspects of it catch your attention. These develop into more specific interests.

In this chapter, we want to begin naming your key interests.

If you aren't sure what subjects excite and engage you, try answering the following questions:

THINGS TO DO, PEOPLE TO SEE, PLACES TO GO

1. What magazines, newspapers, or newsletters do you read? ____________________

____

Which articles attract your attention? ____________________

Which section do you turn to first? ____________________

Which publications do you cherish and wouldn't miss? ____________________

2. What kind of movies do you like? (check your preferences)

- ❍ mystery
- ❍ action/adventure
- ❍ science fiction/supernatural
- ❍ family
- ❍ love/romance
- ❍ comedy
- ❍ other ____________

What do you like about that type of movie? ______________________

____

3. What other forms of entertainment do you like and why? (check your preferences)

- ❍ radio
- ❍ theater
- ❍ dance clubs
- ❍ restaurants
- ❍ amusement parks
- ❍ concerts
- ❍ outdoor events/camping/hiking
- ❍ sports
- ❍ video games
- ❍ parties

Other ______________________

4. How do you like to spend your free time? ______________________

____

5. Whose company do you most enjoy? (peers? older adults? children? variety of ages? animals?)

____

6. What groups (if any) do you presently belong to or would you like to belong to? (clubs, teams, volunteer groups, extracurricular activities) ______________________

____

7. Which individuals do you admire? Who are your role models? (teachers, business people, politicians, athletes, historical figures) ______________________

What is it about these people that you admire? ______________________

8. What environments do you like?

❍ computers
❍ machinery
❍ transportation—airplanes, trains, buses, cars, space travel
❍ travel destinations
❍ museums—art, history, science
❍ government—courts, firefighters, police, sanitation, legal system
❍ entertainment—movies, live theater, concerts
❍ fashion
❍ shopping
❍ nature—mountains, desert, forest, beach
❍ sports—playing or observing
❍ animals
❍ farms

INTEREST INVENTORY: PASSIONS FROM A–Z

Read the following list of interests and rate your interest for each item. **No interest** = you don't care about the subject area and don't want to know more about it. **Some interest** = you are curious about the subject and spend some time focusing on it. **Strong interest** = you are very interested in the subject and enjoy spending time learning about it.

❶ No interest ❷ Some interest ❸ Strong interest

acting	①	②	③	art	①	②	③
action/adventure	①	②	③	ballet	①	②	③
agriculture	①	②	③	bargains	①	②	③
airplanes	①	②	③	beauty	①	②	③
animals	①	②	③	being first	①	②	③
antiques	①	②	③	boats	①	②	③
architecture	①	②	③	body building	①	②	③

❶ No interest	❷ Some interest	❸ Strong interest					
body shaping	①	②	③	current events	①	②	③
books	①	②	③	cutting	①	②	③
buildings	①	②	③	dance, ballet	①	②	③
buses	①	②	③	dance, modern	①	②	③
business	①	②	③	dance, ballroom	①	②	③
cameras	①	②	③	decorating	①	②	③
cars	①	②	③	design	①	②	③
chess	①	②	③	disabilities	①	②	③
children	①	②	③	driving	①	②	③
clay	①	②	③	ecology	①	②	③
clothing	①	②	③	education	①	②	③
color	①	②	③	elderly people	①	②	③
communication	①	②	③	English	①	②	③
computers	①	②	③	entertainment	①	②	③
concerts, classical	①	②	③	ethnicity	①	②	③
concerts, rock	①	②	③	environmental protection	①	②	③
concerts, jazz	①	②	③	evolution	①	②	③
cooking	①	②	③	exercise	①	②	③
cosmetics	①	②	③	exports/imports	①	②	③
costumes	①	②	③	fabric	①	②	③
creating environments	①	②	③	fame	①	②	③

	❶ No interest	❷ Some interest	❸ Strong interest
farming	①	②	③
fashion	①	②	③
fixing things	①	②	③
fixtures	①	②	③
flowers	①	②	③
food	①	②	③
foreign cultures	①	②	③
foreign languages	①	②	③
furniture	①	②	③
gardening	①	②	③
hand tools	①	②	③
healing	①	②	③
health	①	②	③
helping others	①	②	③
history	①	②	③
human anatomy	①	②	③
human potential	①	②	③
human psychology	①	②	③
humor	①	②	③
illness	①	②	③
images	①	②	③
infants	①	②	③
intellectual challenges	①	②	③
interior design	①	②	③
international affairs	①	②	③
jazz	①	②	③
jewelry	①	②	③
language, use & structure	①	②	③
law	①	②	③
leadership	①	②	③
learning	①	②	③
lighting	①	②	③
listening to music	①	②	③
listening to people's stories	①	②	③
machinery	①	②	③
martial arts	①	②	③
mathematics	①	②	③
mechanical challenges	①	②	③
mediating	①	②	③
medicine	①	②	③
money	①	②	③
movement	①	②	③

❶ No interest ❷ Some interest ❸ Strong interest

movies	①	②	③
music, classical	①	②	③
music, jazz	①	②	③
music, rock	①	②	③
music composition	①	②	③
musical instruments	①	②	③
nature	①	②	③
natural products	①	②	③
negotiating	①	②	③
nutrition	①	②	③
observing	①	②	③
packaging	①	②	③
painting	①	②	③
party planning	①	②	③
peace	①	②	③
people	①	②	③
performing	①	②	③
personal appearance	①	②	③
philosophy	①	②	③
physical work	①	②	③
plants	①	②	③
plays	①	②	③
pottery	①	②	③
poetry	①	②	③
politics	①	②	③
public speaking	①	②	③
reading	①	②	③
recipes	①	②	③
recycling	①	②	③
relationships	①	②	③
religion	①	②	③
research	①	②	③
retail stores	①	②	③
sculpture	①	②	③
sign language	①	②	③
scent	①	②	③
science	①	②	③
sewing	①	②	③
shopping	①	②	③
singing	①	②	③
sleeping	①	②	③
sound	①	②	③

❶ No interest ❷ Some interest ❸ Strong interest			
shoes	①	②	③
speech	①	②	③
spirituality	①	②	③
sports	①	②	③
stock market	①	②	③
stones	①	②	③
style	①	②	③
teaching	①	②	③
technology	①	②	③
telephone	①	②	③
television	①	②	③
texture	①	②	③
theater	①	②	③
toys	①	②	③
trade	①	②	③
travel	①	②	③
trees	①	②	③
trends	①	②	③
unusual objects	①	②	③
video	①	②	③
walking	①	②	③
wiring	①	②	③
wood	①	②	③
words	①	②	③
working with hands	①	②	③
writing	①	②	③
zoology	①	②	③
other interests:			
______________	①	②	③
______________	①	②	③
______________	①	②	③
______________	①	②	③
______________	①	②	③

Now look at your 3s. Select the top five interests that you would like to include in your work life.

Interests I Want to Include in My Work Life

1. ______________________________

2. ______________________________

3. ______________________________

4. ______________________________

5. ______________________________

Congratulations! You've just completed your Interests Inventory. We'll be using your five strongest interests to further clarify your indie business idea. The next chapter will address the final phase of self-assessment, personal lifestyle preferences. Before you turn to chapter 8, look over the talent/skills/interests profiles of our twelve indie professionals. See if any of their combinations looks similar to yours.

Profession: Actor

Talents:		**Skills:**	
	Powers of concentration		Acting techniques
	Physical stamina		Dance
	Entertain people		Movement techniques
	Ability to empathize		Public speaking
	Word memory		Voice, singing & speaking

Strong Interests: performing, human psychology, plays, movies, theater

---

Profession: Advertising Consultant

Talents:		**Skills:**	
	Identify trends		Advertising writing
	Generate and develop ideas		Art direction
	Express ideas		Marketing
	Ability with words		Psychological development
	Persuade people		Typography

Strong interests: words, writing, reading, human psychology, trends, business

---

Profession: Caterer

Talents:
- Ability to cook
- Physical stamina
- Sense of composition
- Set up systems for getting things done
- Manage people

Skills:
- Cooking techniques
- Food preparation
- Food presentation
- Nutrition
- Time management

Strong interests: food, recipes, cooking, entertaining, party planning

---

Profession: Computer Programmer

Talents:
- Think logically
- Analyze facts and ideas
- Break things down into smaller units
- See steps to achieving goals
- Analyze and solve problems

Skills:
- Computer science
- Computer languages
- Computer operating systems
- Computer programming
- Mathematics

Strong interests: math, intellectual challenges, computers, science, learning

---

Profession: Computer Technician

Talents:
- Assemble things & take things apart
- Diagnose mechanical problems
- Use hand tools
- Operate equipment
- Analyze and solve problems

Skills:
- Computer science
- Computer wiring & networking
- Machine maintenance & repair
- Electrical wiring
- Computer operation systems

Strong interests: fixing things, computers, hand tools, machinery, mechanical challenges

---

Profession: Fashion Designer

Talents:
- Forecast trends
- Attend to details
- Assemble things
- Sense of style & composition
- Color perception & sense of texture

Skills:
- Merchandising
- Pattern making
- Sewing
- Illustration
- Clothing design

Strong interests: fashion, beauty, body shape, color & fabric, trends

---

Profession: Graphic Designer

Talents:
Ability to work alone
Generate and develop ideas
Spatial perception
Sense of composition
Analyze and solve problems

Skills:
Typography
Graphic design
Art direction
Drawing
Desktop publishing

Strong interests: art, packaging, color, design, intellectual challenges

---

Profession: Lawyer

Talents:
Think logically
Gather information & data
Retain information
Mediate, resolve conflict
Ability with words

Skills:
Law
Legal writing
Legal systems
Negotiation
Public speaking

Strong Interests: reading, language, negotiating, history, learning

---

Profession: Personal Trainer

Talents:
Good physical coordination & stamina
Listen attentively
Analyze and solve problems
Motivate & teach people
Help others

Skills:
Anatomy
Physiology
First aid and CPR
Kinesthesiology
Fitness training

Strong interests: exercise, health, human anatomy, people, personal appearance

---

Profession: Psychotherapist

Talents:
Empathize
Help others
Perceive/define cause & effect relationships
Listen attentively
Handle emotional crises

Skills:
Abnormal psychology
Psychological development
Clinical psychology
Psychological assessment
Theories of psychiatric intervention

Strong interests: human psychology, human potential, relationships, listening to people's stories, observing

---

Profession:	Restaurateur		
Talents:	Attend to other people's needs	**Skills:**	Accounting
	Physical stamina		Management
	Set up systems for getting things done		Marketing
	Attend to details		Purchasing
	Ability to multitask		Food preparation

Strong interests: people, food, entertaining, physical work, creating environments

---

Profession:	Video Producer		
Talents:	Remain calm under pressure	**Skills:**	Film production
	Generate and develop ideas		Film editing
	Spatial perception		Lighting
	Sense of timing & composition		Management
	Plan projects & attend to details		Business writing

Strong interests: images, words, camera, art, film, business

---

chapter 8
CHOOSING YOUR LIFESTYLE

Paul R. graduated from an east coast law school eager to launch a new life. Growing up in the industrial Northeast, he'd always dreamed about living on the west coast, enjoying the mountains, rivers, and fresh air. After checking out his options, Paul set his sights for Seattle, Washington. He knew that Seattle was a thriving city with plenty of outdoor activities. He researched Seattle's legal market and discovered that Seattle needed divorce lawyers and conflict mediation specialists. Paul had studied both of these topics in law school and felt qualified to offer his expertise to prospective clients. Paul could work in Seattle and enjoy a healthy, athletic lifestyle. He spent the summer preparing for his move and studying for the bar exam.

After Paul passed the bar exam in Seattle, he set up his indie law practice. Because he wanted to work from home, Paul looked for a centrally located apartment that could double as living space and home office. He found just the right space in downtown Seattle, and moved in on September 1.

Paul didn't want to share office space with other lawyers, but he did want to build a network of legal colleagues. He also wanted to meet other professionals with whom he could share referrals and exchange information. Paul joined the local lawyers' association, and attended meetings at the Chamber of Commerce.

Over the next six months, Paul took many actions to meet people and advertise his services. He worked hard to build a solid client base, but he also designed his work life so that he could take Friday afternoons and weekends off. Though Paul wanted to make a decent living through his law practice, he was equally committed to enjoying the outdoors and staying physically active.

Your Business Should Fit Your Lifestyle

The information age has given us new lifestyle choices. Before computers and other forms of mobile technology became commonplace, it was necessary for people to work in central locations where they could exchange information and where the mass production of goods and services could take place. Today, information and resources can be exchanged easily from many locations. Products can be manufactured overseas or locally. It is no longer necessary to work in a prescribed setting.

Take advantage of these technological changes to define the kind of lifestyle you want to live, and design your indie venture around it. Like Paul R., you can decide where you want to live, what hours you want to work, and what kind of setting you want to work in. Indies don't need to work in office buildings—they can work from home. Indies don't need to be in one specific city or town—they can do business from almost any location—city, suburb, or rural area. Indies don't have to dress in corporate attire every day. They can dress casually or formally, depending on the situation.

Smart indies incorporate their lifestyle preferences into their business ideas. They make sure that they work in a geographic setting that fits them; a place where they can pursue their interests and live a satisfying life. As you begin to design your indie career, it's important to clarify what kind of lifestyle you want to create.

The following questionnaire will help you explore your lifestyle preferences in eight big areas. Write your responses to each of the questions, and see what kind of lifestyle emerges. Following the questionnaire, you will find two sample questionnaires showing the responses of indies who designed businesses with their lifestyle preferences in mind.

LIFESTYLE PREFERENCES

1. **Geographic location**

   What kind of work environment do you prefer?

   ❍ Home ❍ Office building ❍ Other

   ❍ City ❍ Suburbs ❍ Rural

2. **People**

   What kind of people do you want to work with? ________

   Do you prefer working with others or by yourself? ________

Whom do you want as a customer or client? ___

3. Hours

How many hours a week do you want to work? ___

How many months a year? ___

4. Stress level

How much stress are you willing to endure? ___

5. Income

How much money do you want to earn? ___

6. Family/friends

Who in your life needs to fit into your business? ___

7. Religious beliefs/spiritual practices

What ethics, morals, and values cannot be compromised? ___

How should your business incorporate your religious beliefs and spiritual practices? ___

8. Personal requirements

What other personal requirements are involved? ___

Health considerations ___

Hobbies ___

Special needs ___

SAMPLE RESPONSES

Sharon B.— Graphic designer

1. **Geographic location—Chicago**

   What kind of work environmentally do you prefer?

   ❍ Home | ☒ Office building | ❍ Other
   ☒ City | ❍ Suburbs | ❍ Rural

2. **People**

   What kind of people do you want to work with? **I want to have a cooperative office in which I share space with other business owners—copywriters, package designers, public relations consultants, and advertising consultants. We can refer work to each other.**

   Do you prefer working with others or by yourself? **I prefer working by myself, but I like having contact with other people during the day.**

   Whom do you want as a customer or client? **I'd like to design books and book jacket covers for publishing companies.**

3. **Hours**

   How many hours a week do you want to work? **I'm willing to work 60 hours/week.**

   How many months a year? **I'm willing to work 11 months a year (two-week vacations every 6 months).**

4. **Stress level**

   How much stress are you willing to endure? **I don't mind the stress of deadlines, but I don't** want to be constantly under the gun.

5. **Income**
   How much money do you want to earn? I'd like to earn $40–50,000 per year to start.

6. **Family/friends**
   Who in your life needs to fit into your business? (Children, parents, husband/wife, close friend, brother/sister) I want to live close to my family and have time to see my friends.

7. **Religious beliefs/spiritual practices**
   What ethics and morals and values can not be compromised? I need to work with companies that are honest and forthright in their dealings with me. I cannot do anything illegal in terms of copying existing designs or stealing design ideas from other people.

   How should your business incorporate your religious beliefs and spiritual practices? Because I am Jewish, my business should respect Jewish holidays and practices. I will not work on a religious holidays or during the Sabbath.

8. **Personal requirements**

   What other personal requirements are involved?

   Health considerations Need an office where no one smokes

   Hobbies Music, running, dance

   Special needs

David G.—Web Page Designer

1. Geographic location—Colorado

What kind of work environmentally do you prefer?

- [x] Home
- [ ] Office building
- [ ] Other
- [ ] City
- [ ] Suburbs
- [x] Rural —**Mountains**

2. People

What kind of people do you want to work with? **People who represent good causes.**

Do you prefer working with others or by yourself? **I prefer working by myself from my home. I can communicate with clients via E-mail and the Internet.**

Whom do you want as a customer or client? **Not-for-profit companies.**

3. Hours

How many hours a week do you want to work? **I'm willing to work 45 hours per week. I want to work flexible hours so I can ski or hike in the mornings. I am willing to work evenings and some weekends.**

How many months a year? **I'm willing to work 11 months a year.**

4. Stress level

How much stress are willing to endure? **I prefer a low-stress environment; that's why I want to work from my home in the mountains.**

5. Income

How much money do you want to earn? **I want to earn $40,000 per year.**

6. Family/friends

Who in your life needs to fit into your business? (Children, parents, husband/wife, close friend, brother/sister) I am a big skier, so I need to have time for my skiing buddies and close friends. Also, I want time to spend time with my girlfriend.

7. Religious beliefs/spiritual practices

What ethics and morals and values can not be compromised? I need to work with companies that pay me on time. I also need to practice honesty and compliance regarding the business agreements I make with my clients. I want to deliver work on time and complete.

How should your business incorporate your religious beliefs and spiritual practices? My business will design web sites for not-for-profits, which fits with my religious beliefs. I am a Buddhist and I believe in work that has purpose and compassion.

8. Personal requirements

What other personal requirements are involved?

Health considerations

Hobbies Skiing, hiking, meditation.

Special needs Office needs to overlook mountains. Also, I want a garden.

chapter 9
FINDING BUSINESS TRENDS AND OPPORTUNITIES

Philip Z. owned a software documentation and training company. During his first ten years of business, Philip targeted Fortune 1000 companies only. Philip's company developed a solid reputation within the corporate world for delivering first-rate software training and documentation.

Philip enjoyed his company's success among large corporations. But he understood that real growth would require expanding into other markets. Philip began looking at the trends shaping software products and training. With a little research, Philip determined that home-based businesses constituted a growing market, and that each of those businesses wanted Internet exposure. So, Philip directed his employees to develop the first "How To Put Up Your Own Web Site" software and handbook.

Philip spotted a trend. He noticed that real growth in his industry was moving away from big business and towards small business. His company now serves both markets.

TARGETING TRENDS

One of the most important skills that successful indies foster is the ability to keep one eye on the future. Like Philip Z., smart indies analyze their industries and identify the **trends.** A trend is a direction of movement. In Philip's example, the fact that more and more people were starting home-based businesses was a trend. Small-business owners' demand for Internet exposure was also a trend. Finally, the fact that small-business owners were becoming the largest consumers of software products and services was another trend. Philip put three trends together, and came up with his product idea—a do-it-yourself Web site kit. Philip's product moved in the direction of opportunity and growth within his industry.

When it comes to picking up on trends, indies have the advantage over big companies. Indies can move quickly to reshape their businesses. Once they identify an area of potential growth within their industry, they can shift gears in that direction.

Deborah G. owned a retail store for women's workout and sports gear. Deborah's clientele consisted of women who participated in organized sports and exercised in health clubs. Deborah's store had a good reputation and a loyal customer base. Still, during her fifth year of business, Deborah noticed that fewer women came by on a daily basis to shop.

Deborah became curious about this and began examining the trends. With careful research, Deborah learned two important things:

1) Because more women now work, raise children, and run households, they are more time-starved and less likely to go shopping.
2) When women do shop, they look for ease and accessibility.

This information helped Deborah to align her sports gear business with current trends. First, she opened retail outlets inside several prominent health clubs so that her customers could have easy access to her goods. Then Deborah produced a catalog that she mailed to more than 5,000 exercising women in her vicinity. Deborah's actions resulted in a 200 percent increase in the sales of her sports gear.

SEIZING OPPORTUNITIES

Opportunities arise when change occurs. With each new invention or lifestyle change, new needs arise. The people who notice and seize opportunities before anyone else does are called "trendsetters." As an indie you may not become a trendsetter, but you'll want to train yourself to capitalize on trends and opportunities.

John T. was in college pursuing a computer science degree. He needed some extra money to upgrade his printer and modem. John lived in a dormitory. At night, John frequently heard his dorm mates—most of whom were business majors—complaining about how long it took them to get technical support for their computers over the phone.

John saw a business opportunity. He realized that he could sell his services as a computer

> consultant to his classmates. John knew how to maintain, program, repair, and upgrade his own computer. He could easily do the same for others. John launched his business and called it J.T. Computrain. He advised, trained, and assisted his fellow classmates on their computers. He set up accounts with individual students whereby they could get technical support from him on a monthly basis for a nominal fee.
>
> By the time John graduated from college, J.T. Computrain had more than thirty customers. John decided to incorporate. He continued to build his client base and even retained many of his first clients after graduation.

We spot trends by paying attention to the past, examining the present, and predicting the future. The future may seem mysterious because it is full of so many unknowns. But the future can be somewhat predictable if you watch for emerging patterns. For example, in social behavior, conservative behavior follows a period of progressive or liberal behavior.

The Fifties were a very conservative time. The end of World War II brought a resurgence of traditional gender roles and traditional family values.

The Sixties were more turbulent. Civil unrest, youthful rebellion, and the Vietnam War were in focus. Hippies embodied the radical behavior of the times.

The Seventies were very radical times—the rebellious attitudes of the sixties continued. Psychedelic drugs, nudity, women's liberation, sexual freedom, divorce, draft dodging, and the "me" generation were highlights of this time.

The Eighties brought a wave of conservatism back into society. We began to clean up; hippies were replaced by yuppies. People began talking about family values again.

The Nineties bring a continuation of the conservatism that appeared in the eighties. Family values have come center stage. Liberal is a dirty word.

What will the year 2000 bring? Based on the past pattern, the conservative trend will continue for at least another ten years, until the pendulum swings in the other direction again.

THREE STEPS FOR IDENTIFYING TRENDS

Step I—Examine the Past

Before you go into any business, do a little research. Find out about the history of your industry. Look at its past to see the patterns of change. Take the food industry, for example. Over the years food has gone from farm-fresh (up to the 1930s) to frozen (in the forties, fifties, and sixties) to fast food (in the sixties, seventies, and eighties) to health-oriented fresh (in the eighties and nineties). Once you examine your prospective industry's past, you can look into the future to see where it's going.

Step II—Imagine the Future

Next take your indie idea and use your imagination. Suspend logical thinking and allow your mind to dream about what could happen. Take your idea and envision where it might go in the future.

Example: A T-shirt
Next Stage: A sun-resistant T-shirt that blocks out sun rays
Next Stage: A sun- and heat-resistant T-shirt that keeps you cool
Next Stage: A sun-, heat-, and cold-resistant T-shirt that also knows when it's cold outside and keeps you warm
Next Stage: An antinuclear jumpsuit, head to toe, that protects you from the environment

(If these examples seem far out to you, they aren't. These products are being produced right now or are in the prototype stage and will probably be available to you in the near future.) Once you imagine how your product or service may evolve over the next few years, you can decide how to design your indie venture so that it can move with that development.

Step III—Look at the Present for Trends-In-Progress

Watch the next five areas to determine the bigger picture of present trends. Changes in any of these areas could affect your product or service no matter what industry you're in.

1. Our economic condition
2. The political position of the time (conservative, liberal, etcetera)
3. Technological changes that will alter the way we do things
4. How we are spending our leisure time
5. What industries are making the most money, hiring, and making the news

Summary of Trend-Targeting Techniques

1. Look back for patterns

2. Look forward for ideas
3. Look at the present for evidence of trends in progress

Before we close this chapter, here is a list of 22 trends that are already in progress. Under each trend, you'll see several indie business ideas. Go over the list and see if any of the business ideas fit in with your profile.

22 TRENDS IN PROGRESS, 101 INDIE BUSINESS IDEAS

1. Rampant and ongoing changes in technology

24-hour technical support
Computer language training schools
Traveling technology repair vans
Traveling technology education and support services
24-hour delivery of equipment

2. Women in the workforce

Child care services
Personal chefs
Eldercare services
Rent-a-Wife services
Home cleaning crews

3. Minorities rise to power

Minority public relations agencies
Minority fundraising
Minority advertising agencies
Cultural diversity training and education
Multicultural marriage counseling

4. The graying of America—longevity

Elder transportation services
Senior money management
Elder entertainment

Retirement communities
Elder community centers

5. **Home-based businesses**
   Business support groups
   Home office furniture products
   Office organizing consultants
   Relaxed business clothing

6. **Telecommuting**
   Time management systems
   Off-site management training
   Instruments for measuring off-site productivity
   Fast delivery services

7. **Mobile communications**
   Mobile data terminals
   Location information centers
   Mobile communication transport gear
   Mobile phone directories

8. **Home shopping via television, computers & catalogues**
   Catalogs on the Internet
   Shopping television shows for hard-to-find products
   Custom buying via computer
   Customized clothing via the Internet
   Supermarket shopping on Internet with immediate delivery

9. **Fast-paced lives**
   Relaxation classes, tapes, videos
   Virtual environments for total peace of mind
   Retreats and spas

Nonreligious spiritual environments for inner peace
Power nap centers

10. Environmental awareness

Ecologically healthy homes
Products made from recycled goods
Waste management
Air purifiers to kill germs
Breathing masks that clean the air

11. International cuisines for everyday consumption

International frozen foods
International fast foods
Multicuisine restaurants and products
International spices and herbs
Highly specialized food catalogs on the Internet

12. Random terrorism

Mobile security systems
Self-defense education
Bulletproof clothing
"Smart" homes
Bodyguard services

13. Long-distance learning

Teleconferencing centers
Learning videos for all ages
Degrees and certification via online schools
Instant translation of courses into other languages via the Internet

14. Quality of life

Minivacation packages
Family entertainment centers
Home spa services

15. Preventive health care

Nutrition counseling
Holistic health products
Homeopathy
Aromatherapy for work and education environments
Home health care

16. Personal growth

Short-term individual, family & marriage counseling
Self-help books, tapes, seminars
Peer support groups
Positive and inspirational movies
Positive and inspirational TV shows

17. Genetic engineering

Genetic counseling
Genetic research
Drugs—synthetic hormones, genes, etcetera
Genetic law

18. Information as a product

Database software companies
Network memberships
Information packaging
Online industry-wide catalogs
Online industry libraries

19. Customer service orientation

Customer relations experts

24-hour service centers

Customer incentive companies

20. Personal services

Personal shoppers

Professional organizers

Personal trainers

Home hairstylists

Home manicures and pedicures

Food delivery

21. Backlash to technology (desire for more human contact)

Massage therapists

Live entertainment in small spaces

Formalized play groups for children and teens

Original handmade products

Neighborhood cafes and clubs

22. Backlash to clean living

Cigar clubs

Casinos and nightclubs

Products loaded with caffeine

Products loaded with sugar

As a business owner, you'll always have one eye on the future. You'll be charting the future of the industry you're in and the future of your own business venture. As your industry cycles through trends, you want to be sure that your own venture keeps up with the changes.

chapter 10
PUTTING IT ALL TOGETHER

So far you've assessed your talents, your skills, your interests, and your lifestyle preferences. You've read about trends, and you've seen 101 of the hottest indie ideas. It's time to put it all together and create your **indie profile**. Your indie profile will summarize all the self-assessment exercises you completed in the previous chapters. It is a single document you can refer to that clearly expresses who you are. It will help you determine the kind of indie work you should do. From your profile, you'll be able to come up with workable, exciting indie ideas that fit your personality and capitalize on your talents and skills.

Take your time putting the profile together. Follow the steps below, read the examples, and make sure you're satisfied with the final version of your diagram. If you want to add any categories or comments to make your profile more accurate, please do.

PUTTING TOGETHER YOUR INDIE PROFILE

1. Begin by turning to page 40 in chapter 5 where you listed your top-five natural talents. On the Indie Profile form below, list them in order of importance to you.
2. Turn to page 54 in chapter 6 where you listed skills you have and want to use at work. Copy those five skills under the same heading on the diagram. Next, take the five skills you want to develop and use at work and list those too.
3. Turn to page 67 of chapter 7, where you listed the top five interests you'd like to include in your work life. Write those five interests under the Strong Interests heading.
4. Finally, go to page 72–74 of chapter 8, where you listed your lifestyle preferences. Transfer the responses you gave to each of those questions to the matching Lifestyle Preference category on the profile form.

When you have completed the profile, turn to the following page, and we can take the next step in finding your indie venture.

INDIE PROFILE

Top Five Natural Talents

1. ______________________
2. ______________________
3. ______________________
4. ______________________
5. ______________________

Skills I Want To Develop and Use At Work

1. ______________________
2. ______________________
3. ______________________
4. ______________________
5. ______________________

Skills I Have and Want To Use At Work

1. ______________________
2. ______________________
3. ______________________
4. ______________________
5. ______________________

Top Five Strong Interests I'd Like to Include in My Work Life

1. ______________________
2. ______________________
3. ______________________
4. ______________________
5. ______________________

Lifestyle Preferences

1. Geographic location

❍ Home ❍ Office building ❍ Other ______________

❍ City ❍ Suburbs ❍ Rural

2. People

____

3. Hours

Hours per week __________ Months a year __________

4. **Stress level**
   ❍ High Stress ❍ Medium Stress ❍ Low Stress ❍ Other ____________

5. **Income** ______________________________

6. **Family/friends**

   Who needs to fit into your business? ____________

7. **Religious beliefs/spiritual practices**

   What ethics, morals, and values cannot be compromised? ____________

   How should your business incorporate religious beliefs and spiritual practices? ____________

8. **Personal requirements**

   Health considerations ____________

   Hobbies ____________

   Special needs ____________

Notes

Now that you have constructed your indie profile, use it to brainstorm about business ideas. Jot your ideas down here:

Indie business ideas that immediately come to mind:

____

____

____

____

Next, turn to chapter 9 and look at the trends. Browse through the 101 indie business ideas. With your indie profile in mind, do any of those business ideas seem like a good match for you? Do you have another business idea that would fall under one of the Trends In Progress? Jot down those indie business ideas here:

Indie business ideas I have that are part of Trends In Progress:

____

____

____

____

Important Note:
Don't worry if you don't come up with a business idea for yourself immediately. This is a process, and you need to give yourself time to look at your profile, show it to others, and play around with different indie business ideas. We suggest you make copies of your indie profile so you can look at it and show it to others for ideas and feedback. Post one copy in your room. Give other copies to friends and family and see if they have ideas for you.

Let's look at how some other indies used their profile to come up with business ideas.

INDIE PROFILE

Name: Kathy L.

Top-Five Natural Talents

1. Relate to wide range of people
2. Listen attentively
3. Set steps to achieving goals
4. Analyzing and solving problems
5. Generating and developing ideas

Skills I Want to Develop and Use at Work

1. Facilitating
2. Interviewing
3. Group dynamics
4. Organizational development
5. Negotiating

Skills That I Have That I Want to Use at Work

1. Business telephone skills
2. Office systems
3. Marketing
4. Sales
5. Time management

Top-Five Strong Interests I'd Like to Include in My Work Life

1. Business
2. Human psychology
3. Helping others
4. Learning
5. Teaching

Lifestyle Preferences

1. Geographic location

- [x] Home
- [ ] Office building
- [ ] Other
- [x] City
- [ ] Suburbs
- [ ] Rural

2. People

I want to work with creative, interesting people. I want to have contact with a lot of people on a weekly basis. I want my customer to be entrepreneurs.

3. Hours

Hours per week *50–60* Months a year **10**

4. Stress level

❍ High Stress ☒ Medium Stress ❍ Low Stress ❍ Other ____________

5. Income $40–50,000

6. Family/friends

Who needs to fit into your business? No one in particular.

7. Religious beliefs/spiritual practices

Ethics/morals/values that can't be compromised I want to work only with ethical people.

Don't want people who rip off me or others .

How should your business incorporate religious beliefs and spiritual practices?

8. Personal requirements

Health considerations None

Hobbies Socializing, cooking, entertaining.

Special needs None

After completing her indie profile, **Kathy L.** was not sure what kind of indie business would fit her. She saw that she had plenty to offer in terms of talents and skills, but she wasn't sure where to go with it all. Then, Kathy went back to chapter 6, and reviewed the 101 Business Ideas. She came across one idea that made sense to her. It was under the trend of Home-Based Businesses. The idea was Business Support Groups.

With her interpersonal talents, business skills, and interest in business and human psychology, Kathy could really enjoy running support groups for the population she enjoyed most—

creative entrepreneurs. Now, Kathy could work on acquiring the information and facilitation skills that would really make her business support groups effective.

INDIE PROFILE

Name: Ryan T.

Top-Five Natural Talents

1. Gathering information and data
2. Thinking logically
3. Strong powers of concentration
4. Analyzing and solving problems
5. Sorting and categorizing

Skills I Want to Develop and Use at Work

1. Computer programming
2. Computer software design
3. Graphic design
4. Editing
5. Marketing

Skills That I Have I Want to Use at Work

1. Operating computer systems
2. Computer maintenance
3. Desktop publishing
4. Word processing
5. Time management

Top-Five Strong Interests I'd Like to Include in My Work Life

1. Intellectual challenges
2. Computers
3. Business
4. Math
5. Technology

Lifestyle Preferences

1. Geographic location

☒ Home ❍ Office building ❍ Other

❍ City ❍ Suburbs ☒ Rural

2. People

I want work that lets me interact with other computer geeks. I want to work by myself at home. I want my customer to be people who use computers and the Internet.

3. Hours

Hours per week *70* Months a year 12

4. **Stress level**
❍ High Stress ❍ Medium Stress ☒ Low Stress ❍ Other ____________

5. **Income** $200,000

6. **Family/friends**

Who needs to fit into your business? **No one in particular.**

7. **Religious beliefs/spiritual practices**

What ethics, morals, and values cannot be compromised? **I won't buy or sell any products that are harmful to the environment. I want to be fair in business.**

Incorporating religious beliefs/spiritual practices **None**

8. **Personal requirements**

Health considerations **None**

Hobbies **Fishing, camping, hiking.**

Special needs **None**

Ryan T. looked at his indie profile and realized he already had a business idea that he could begin to develop now. He'd always wanted to produce an Internet catalog for software products. Ryan constantly read about new software products and applications on his own. An Internet catalog would turn his hobby into a money-making venture.

He told his indie idea to Greg, his best buddy. Greg said it seemed perfect, especially because Ryan could live in a rural area, work from his home, and still earn a living. "It would allow you to live in the boonies while you sold your catalog over the wires."

Your indie business idea may not become evident as quickly as it did for Kathy and Ryan. Still, if you keep your profile in mind and continue to explore different indie business ideas, you'll find a good match eventually.

Finding your indie venture is not a simple task. It might take awhile. Don't give up. Continue reading this book. In the final section, we explore the essential skills you'll need to prosper in your independent business venture. You may get a great idea as you move through the chapters.

chapter 11
TESTING YOUR IDEAS

You've got your business idea. You think it could work as an indie business. Now, it's time to test it. All indie ideas need to be tested. Take Zelda K. from chapter 4. She baked cakes, cookies, pies, and candies as a hobby. Zelda tested out her indie idea by making baked goods for the people she knew. She found out which baked goods enjoyed universal popularity and which did not. She tinkered with her recipes, and perfected her confections.

All through high school, Zelda baked treats for the special events of her family and friends. As the number of requests mounted, she asked for money to cover her expenses. By her junior year, Zelda felt confident enough in her expertise to charge real fees for her baked goods and begin paying herself. Her indie venture had been launched.

Let's revisit Clara G., the dog walker from chapter 3 who grew her business by passing out flyers. Clara's indie idea was born on her fourteenth birthday. That's when Clara got a golden retriever as a present from her grandparents. While training her dog, Clara saw that she had a special talent for working with canines. She started testing her indie idea when she began volunteering to take care of her neighbors' dogs when they were away. She developed a reputation as a dog expert, and neighbors began requesting her dog sitting and dog walking services. These early experiences fed into Clara's business venture.

Indie ideas can be tested long before they become full-time businesses. If you don't test out your idea, you could set yourself up for a fall. Testing your idea can help you avoid the most common pitfalls of new indie ventures.

Let's take a closer look at how to navigate around these hazards.

Top Indie Business Pitfalls

1. Assuming you've got a great product or service before anyone tries it.
2. Not having the experience you need in your industry or profession.
3. Not knowing the financial facts of your business.
4. Not having an experienced mentor to get teach you through the unknowns.

ASSUMING YOU'VE GOT A GREAT PRODUCT OR SERVICE BEFORE ANYONE TRIES IT

Joyce S. was a natural-material girl. She wore natural-fiber clothes, ate fresh foods, and used herbs for medication and skin care. As part of her all-natural regime, Joyce created her own moisturizer that had no preservatives and kept her skin very soft. She also formulated a facial scrub that was all-natural. It left her skin cleansed and refreshed. Joyce infused her scrub with the scent of tropical flowers.

Joyce gave sample jars to several friends and asked for feedback. Her friends expressed a wide range of reactions to both products. The feedback they gave was honest and helpful. For example, Joyce learned that texture was important to some people. They wanted a scrub that was effective but didn't feel too thick or grainy. Also, smell was key. Her friends didn't want anything that smelled too pungent.

Joyce adjusted her products to fit her friends' specifications. She then sent the revised moisturizer and facial scrub to a larger sample audience (45 people). With each sample packet, Joyce enclosed a questionnaire. For the next three months, Joyce gathered feedback and continued to improve her formulas. Within one year, most of Joyce's experimenters became paying clients. She'd been able to test her products and obtain new customers simultaneously.

Joyce's story clearly illustrates the value of testing out a product or service before taking it to the general public. If Joyce had not tested her skin remedies before deciding on the final formulas, she could have produced cases of skin cream and facial scrub that no one wanted to use. The sooner you test your idea, the sooner you'll learn what may be wrong with it. Customers who sample your product or service during the testing phase are more likely to give you honest feedback on how to improve it. By trying out your indie idea on small audiences, you can find out what the bugs are, figure out how to solve them, and eventually turn your idea into a full-fledged business.

NOT HAVING THE EXPERIENCE YOU NEED IN YOUR INDUSTRY OR PROFESSION

Diana B. was fascinated with fashion. She wanted to design and sell her original line of clothing. In her spare time, she made up samples of the pants, vests, and skirts that were her trademark. Diane took her samples around to stores, hoping that someone would give her an order. What she quickly found out was that she lacked critical experience.

The store owners wanted better fabrics. Diana didn't know where to buy these. They wanted their orders to be delivered within two weeks. Diana didn't even have a place where she could get her garments made. And the buyers wanted Diana to make some of her design concepts less dramatic and more standard. She didn't want to do that.

Diana realized that she wasn't ready to run a clothing design business. Her knowledge gaps were too big. She decided that her best option would be to work for an established fashion company to learn the ropes of the industry. Through her college, Diana secured an internship with a prominent fashion design company. Diana could learn how the company worked in exchange for five hours of clerical work a week. The head designer would be available to Diana for two hours a week to teach her the ins and outs of fashion.

Like Diana, you may not have the experience you need to work effectively in a certain industry. But like Diana, you also have options. Smart indies find ways to obtain the experience they need for their business venture in a variety of ways—internships, part-time work, intensive courses, mentor programs. (We'll go into each of these learning options in more detail further on in this chapter.)

NOT KNOWING THE FINANCIAL FACTS OF YOUR BUSINESS

The expansion of **Ron T.'s** bicycle delivery service was in high gear. Each week he added ten new customers. Ron had no problem finding delivery jobs. But he didn't seem to be making money. He charged the same fees as his competitors and *they* seemed to be doing well. Ron didn't know what the problem was.

Realizing he might be missing some key information, Ron signed up for a small-business finance course at the local community college. Within two classes, he figured out what the problem was. His cost of doing business was higher than his income. Until he reduced his costs, Ron's company would never make any money. Ron needed to take time out, go back to school and learn something he'd never studied before—small-business finance.

Ron's story is a very common one. Some indies are great at getting business, but don't know the financial facts when it comes to keeping records and making profits. Indie ventures require a lot of hard work and commitment, so you want to make sure that whatever you do, you know how to make it profitable. Knowing and learning the financial facts of small business will save you time and money—before and after you launch your indie venture.

Five Ways To Gain Experience & Test Out Your Indie Idea

1. On-Campus Business Ventures
2. Internships
   - paid/not paid
   - credit/noncredit
3. Mentoring
4. Part-Time Work
5. Education (short-term, specific training)

NOT HAVING A MENTOR TO GET YOU THROUGH THE UNKNOWNS

When **Tommy S.** was turned down for the second time for a bank loan for his new invention, he didn't know where to turn. His banker, Ms. Thrift, felt sorry for Tommy and suggested he speak to a successful business owner for advice. She set up a meeting with Tommy and a local entrepreneur who agreed to advise Tommy on how to get money. The business owner didn't want to get paid for his advice. He only wanted to help a new business owner find his way the same way someone had helped him. He showed Tommy how to create profit and loss statements, and how to write a business plan that investors would take seriously. Within a year, Tommy successfully located a private investor who also served as a financial advisor and consultant as Tommy developed his invention and prepared it for the commercial market.

Mentors are important figures to successful indies. Especially during the early stages of building an indie venture, mentors can offer advice, expertise, and support as you grapple with the many new challenges of your indie career. Like Tommy S., you can find a mentor who is older than you, more experienced than you, and willing to help you develop your indie idea. A good mentor has the expertise and knowledge to help you navigate the unknown areas of your indie career.

HOW TO GAIN EXPERIENCE AND TEST OUT YOUR INDIE IDEA

Here are our five best strategies for looking before you leap into your indie venture.

On-Campus Business Ventures

An excellent way to test your business idea is to start it on a small basis while you're attending school. The cost of running a business on-campus should be low. Marketing your indie product or service should be fairly easy because you have a captive audience (the students). Most important, you'll get an immediate idea regarding the viability of your product or service.

On-campus indie businesses work if your product/service is geared to the student population. If not, you can still test your idea while in school. One option would be to use your business idea as a term project in one of your classes. That way you can solicit the help of your classmates and draw on your professor's expertise.

Internships

Internships are a great way to gain experience, learn an industry, and build your credentials without having a job. Internships are the American way of educating young people about business. When you work as an intern, you have the opportunity to experience first-hand business attitudes, policies, work habits, and systems. You can also learn specific skills.

Internships begin as time-limited assignments. You may intern for a particular company for a semester, a summer, or a year. Internships can develop into something more permanent. They give the employer time to see your skills and abilities. They give you time to really check out a particular industry or company without any strings attached.

Internships are designed specifically for students or young professionals. They usually involve flexible hours that allow for a student's schedule. There is an understanding between the intern and the company that the intern will provide a certain number of work hours and perform clerical or manual tasks. In return, the intern will be exposed to business operations and will be given a business education. Internships work for both parties because companies also get free help.

Internships come in several forms:

- Work in exchange for education
- Work in exchange for education and education credits (some colleges arrange these kinds of internships)
- Work in exchange for education and a small salary or stipend (these are harder to find)

Most colleges have some kind of internship program. You can find out what's available at your school by checking with your placement office, career services bureau, or department head. Internships also exist outside of school. For example, many people in broadcast media begin their careers as interns at major T.V. and radio stations.

Mentoring

Finding a mentor is another way to get high quality education from experts for free. Mentors can be found among experienced business people who have succeeded in reaching their goals. They now have the time to help someone just starting out. Mentors do not perceive their young understudies as threats because they have already made it and just "want to give back."

Mentors are sometimes available through the Small Business Administration. Check into your local SBA. You may also find a mentor through family, friends, or your local chamber of commerce. You may also want to check with college alumnae groups or just ask someone you admire.

Part-Time Work

An excellent way to learn about an industry is to get a part-time job within it and learn from the inside. You can work part time and still go to school. Be careful not to take a job that won't expose you to what you want to learn. For instance, if you want to open a restaurant but don't know how restaurants prepare and distribute multiple meals, get hired as a waiter, waitress, or dishwasher. Find any job that will expose you to the kitchen. Don't take a job in the front of the house as a host, hostess, or bartender. Working part-time will also tell you if you like the industry and help you decide whether you want to go further.

Short-Term Education

Another way of testing your idea is to take short-term classes on practical business-related topics. You can take a one-day or weekend seminar that focuses on the How-To's of starting your particular indie business. In addition, most colleges have continuing education divisions that offer courses taught by industry experts. Here are some examples of short-term courses:

Marketing and Promoting Your Business
Law For Small Businesses
How To Start A Consulting Business
How To Open Your Own Restaurant
Small Business Finance
How To Become An Interior Designer
Starting Your Own Multimedia Company
Selling Your Photographs For Profit

Courses such as these are excellent ways to tap into concrete information and solid business resources. In addition, you may find a mentor in your teacher, or find ways to secure an internship. Short-term education will give you specific and direct answers to your questions.

Testing, Testing . . .

Testing is a must. Once you have an idea for a business venture, be sure to use a combination of methods we just reviewed to gain experience and get the bugs out before you set up a full-time business. If you don't take the time to test your ideas now, then consider your first two to three years in business as your education and testing period.

section **3**

essential
SKILLS

chapter 12
SELF-MANAGEMENT

Donna S. is a copywriter, specializing in brochures, press releases, advertising print, and newsletters for small businesses. Every weekday, Donna is up at 6:45 A.M. She exercises, showers, eats breakfast, and is at her home-office desk by 8:30 A.M. Donna's first task is to organize herself by planning out her day. Her calendar already has the day's appointments on it, and she now schedules time for the other things she wants to accomplish. Donna is careful to schedule non-client-related activities before 9 A.M. and after 5 P.M. After she prioritizes her day, Donna does some writing for a client she'll see in the afternoon. By 9:30 A.M., she has completed her writing task, and is ready to begin contacting clients.

Self-employment liberates you from certain traditional job structures—no boss, no office building, no designated work schedule. Sound terrific? Here's the downside. The lack of structure leaves you a lot of room for relaxing right into bad work habits. Smart indies know the importance of building structure into their work days. They know they require more structure than traditional workers. The self-employed individual's daily plan and work schedule serve as the foundation upon which he or she builds success. Clearly, since you're going to be your own boss, you'll need to learn how to manage yourself effectively.

You've already practiced some form of self-management in school. By the time you reach high school, you know what's expected of you and how to maneuver through the school system. You know what it takes to complete your assignments. You know which subjects are easy for you and which are difficult. If you manage your time well and focus your efforts, you probably do well. If you use your time poorly and scatter your attention, your grades and performance probably suffer.

One way to predict how well you'll manage yourself as an indie is to look at how you manage yourself as a student or employee. Answer the following questions honestly and see what they tell you.

SELF-MANAGEMENT POP QUIZ

When I work or study, I am . . .

(a) able to concentrate on the work I am doing
(b) easily distracted

Faced with a difficult assignment, I . . .

(a) find ways to master the material and complete the assignment
(b) give up and put it aside

When I write a report or term paper, I . . .

(a) complete it early so that I have plenty of time to improve it
(b) wait until the last minute to write it

In general, I hand my assignments in . . .

(a) on time
(b) late

I tend to . . .

(a) remember what I have to do
(b) forget what I have to do

I generally . . .

(a) stay on track with my assignments
(b) fall behind

I usually . . .

(a) plan my social activities around my work
(b) let my social plans come first

You guessed it. The B response for each of these questions indicates an area in which your self-management skills need a little boosting.

ORGANIZING YOUR WORK

Self-Management Basics

1. Organizing your work
2. Managing your time
3. Coaching yourself through obstacles

By organizing your work, you create a structure from which you can operate. Organizing your work involves several steps.

First, set weekly goals. Decide what you want to accomplish by the end of the week. List all of the activities that will be required to achieve those results.

Donna S., Copywriter   Weekly Goals 6/1

1. Work assignments—Finish brochure project for client
   Activities: Finish second draft of brochure copy, fax to client, get corrections, send final draft, collect payment

2. Business development—Mail out 150 newsletters
   Activities: Address 150 newsletters, buy postage, mail out

3. Office organization—Update filing
   Activities: Take pile of papers from desk, sort by subject, put in file cabinet

4. Sales—Make 25 calls; get one new client
   Activities: make five sales calls per day

5. Financial—File bank loan papers with bank
   Activities: Fill out bank loan papers, drop off with loan officer

Second, set priorities—decide which of your goals is the most important. Based on that, decide which activities you should do first.

Priority List

1. Filing (I can't see the bottom of my desk)
2. Finishing client's brochure project (deadline is approaching)
3. Making sales calls for new business (need more immediate business)
4. Filing for bank loan (need capital for expansion in the next year)
5. Sending out newsletters (good for future business development)

Third, make a plan. After you prioritize your activities list, write out a plan for the week. Make an activity list for each day.

	Mon.	Tues.	Wed.	Thur.	Fri.
9 A.M.	file	brochure to proofreader	file	file	file
10 A.M.	write brochure	sales calls	sales calls	sales calls	sales calls
11 A.M.					
12 P.M.		file (30 min.)		get brochure back from proofreader	drop forms at bank
1 P.M.					
2 P.M.	address and mail 50 newsletters		address and mail 50 newsletters	address and mail 50 newsletters	
3 P.M.					finish copy for brochure
4 P.M.	Bank loan papers		Bank loan papers		
5 P.M.					
6 P.M.					

Set at least one major objective for each day and commit yourself to achieving it. Organize your days to make sure you accomplish the most important things first.

MANAGING YOUR TIME

Time is measurable. We all have the same 24 hours a day, yet not everyone manages his or her time effectively. As an indie, your ability to manage your time well will be a key ingredient to your success. There are five basic rules for good time management.

1. **Use a calendar/appointment book**—The busier you are, the more activities you'll schedule into your day. And the more activities you schedule, the more likely you will be to forget or double-book appointments. A calendar and/or a date book is a simple, sound investment for individuals.

2. **Always be on time**—Showing up on time for appointments and events is an extremely important habit for every individual to develop. Your punctuality will be viewed by potential customers and clients as an indication of your reliability and professionalism. Being late will make you look

inconsiderate and unprofessional.

3. **Be sure that the first hour of your work day is productive**—The first hour of work often sets the tone for the rest of your day. If you make sure to use that first hour productively, you'll feel focused and energized for the rest of the day. If you goof off or distract yourself by talking to friends, you'll have a hard time refocusing.

4. **Learn how long it takes for you to complete certain tasks and then give yourself that amount of time**—A common mistake new indies make is to underestimate how long they really need to accomplish certain tasks. For example, a freelance editor may set aside one hour for an editing job that really takes her two hours to complete. Successful indies monitor their time—they see how long it really takes them to accomplish a task from start to finish. Then, they build that amount of time into their schedule. (This skill requires practice; don't worry if it's difficult at first.)

5. **Know your internal clock**—Your internal clock is the mechanism inside you that gives you different levels of energy during the day. Larks (early birds) feel most focused and energetic during the early morning hours. Night owls concentrate and create best during the evening hours. Do you know how your internal clock works? When are you most productive? When are you most creative? What is the best time of day or night for you to tackle difficult problems? When is it difficult for you to focus your energies?

Learn to listen to your internal clock. Plan your day around your metabolic peaks and valleys. Smart indies try to do their most challenging and important work during their high-energy hours. They save their filing for when their batteries are low.

EXPLORING YOUR RELATIONSHIP TO TIME

What is your relationship to time? Is time your friend or your adversary? Does time pass slowly or quickly for you? Do you know where your time goes—or does it just slip away? Your relationship to time has a profound effect on your day-to-day experience as an indie. Here are several common approaches to time. Can you identify with any of them?

"Time Is a Tireless Taskmaster"

Attitude towards time: Very serious, relentless

Behavior: Expect to *always* use time constructively. Spend time constantly working, never relaxing. Unable to give yourself down time or pampering. Have great difficulty setting aside time for fun, vacation, smelling the flowers.

Emotional state: Burdened, tense, heavy

"Your Time is More Important than Mine"

Attitude towards time: Unfocused, undeserving

Behavior: Spend more time than you want meeting other people's needs. Have difficulty saying no to requests/demands from others. Put aside your plans and projects because others need you.

Emotional State: Tired, drained, resentful

"Time Should Give Me Special Treatment"

Attitude towards time: Demanding, willful

Behavior: Consistently underestimate how long it takes to accomplish things. Pack in "extra" activities that make you late for appointments and events. Expect time to speed up or slow down for you. (It takes most people one hour to get to the airport, but YOU should get there in 30 minutes.)

Emotional state: Agitated, rushed, frustrated

"Time Is On My Side"

Attitude towards time: Respectful, grounded

Behavior: Make and consistently pursue long-range plans. Arrive early for appointments. Make promises according to realistic assessment of time involved. Incorporate delays into project timelines. Reserve time for fun and rejuvenation.

Emotional state: Calm, centered, steady

COACHING YOURSELF THROUGH OBSTACLES

All indies face obstacles on the road to success: A desktop publisher's printer may break down just as he's racing to meet a deadline. A personal trainer may suffer a physical injury that impedes her ability to work with clients. A talented computer consultant may not have any customers because he's afraid to make sales calls.

Successful indies understand that they'll experience obstacles to their business and career goals. They don't let those obstacles prevent them from moving forward. They learn how to coach themselves through any barriers to their success. They overcome difficulties by seeking assistance and finding solutions.

Practical Obstacles—Unacquired Business Skills

As a self-employed individual, you'll need to learn a wide range of business skills—goal setting, business planning, office organization, marketing, sales, time management, bookkeeping, etcetera. A business area that you're deficient in or tend to avoid presents an obstacle. If you don't know how to make a sales call to a potential customer or client, your lack of knowledge about selling presents a major obstacle to your success. Similarly, if you avoid keeping accurate records of your income and expenses, your avoidance of bookkeeping impedes your financial clarity and success.

Once you identify a business area you lack skill in or tend to avoid you can seek assistance in mastering it. For example, if you don't know how to make a sales call, you can hire a sales coach, read books about the art of selling, and/or attend a sales training seminar.

If you don't know how to . . .	You can . . .
Write a brochure	Hire a copywriter
Negotiate a business contract	Consult a lawyer
Keep accurate financial records	Work with a bookkeeper
Purchase a computer	Talk to a computer whiz
Sell your product or service	Attend a sales training
Speak in front of large audiences	Take public speaking lessons

You can identify the business skills you don't have and find the help you need to learn them. Remember that successful indies are not born with business expertise. Many have very little formal business training. They are committed, however, to learning whatever skills they need to make their indie enterprise thrive.

Inner Roadblocks

If you're like a lot of people, you may have beliefs, feelings, and attitudes that could get in the way of your success as an indie. Self-employed people have to take a lot of actions to generate their own work, manage their own finances, and monitor their own time. Inner roadblocks can stop you from taking the steps necessary to achieve success.

Five Common Inner Roadblocks to Success

1. **Waiting to be discovered**

   Waiting to be discovered is a common fantasy among new indies. The hope is that instead of having to reach out, contact people, and ask for business, you will be magically discovered by the rich and famous. You will enjoy immediate fame and fortune. The truth is very few people are ever suddenly "discovered."

   The problem with waiting to be discovered is that it prevents you from taking concrete steps towards realizing your own work and career goals. For example, rather than contacting the companies where you want to get hired as a computer programming consultant, you "wait" and hope that they will find you. Meanwhile, you aren't making any money and your indie career is going nowhere.

   The remedy for this inner roadblock is to set weekly goals that reflect your long-term desires, and take concrete actions every week to make your dreams come true.

2. **Impostor belief**

   Many new indies suffer from the impostor belief—they feel that they are not really qualified to do the kind of work that they want to do. They are afraid that they will be exposed by others as an impostor or a fraud.

   The impostor belief inhibits people from putting their work out into the world. You can overcome the impostor belief by simply taking small steps towards overcoming your fears. For example, if you want to start a business as a personal chef but you aren't sure you have enough cooking expertise, you can take some cooking courses and offer your services to three friends. If they like the food you prepare, you can have them write you letters of recommendation that you can give to potential paying customers.

3. **I shouldn't get paid for what I do; it's easy for me**

   This belief usually crops up among indies who are extremely talented and love their work.

The problem is that if you don't charge adequately for your product or service, you won't be able to make a good living on your indie income.

There are several actions you can take to overcome this particular inner roadblock. First, find out what your competitors charge. Do you charge much less than other indies for your product or service? If so, why not raise your fees so that they're at least comparable to your competitors?

Next, if you know that it's hard for you to charge people for your product or service, write your fees down on paper. Having a price list will help you stick to your guns when a potential customer or client wants to underpay you. You can also meet with an accountant and ask for help in determining the appropriate fee structure for your indie enterprise.

4. **Fear of failure**

   Many indies fear failure when they first start out. They imagine that no one will want to hire them or buy their product. They picture themselves penniless, out on the streets.

   Paralysis is the most common symptom. An indie who experiences fear of failure can't make decisions or take actions to generate business. He or she says no to suggestions or ideas about how to move forward.

   You can overcome this inner roadblock by setting goals for your business, and taking small steps every day towards those goals. You can also calm the fear by talking to indies who have more experience than you. Ask them how they got through the early years of pursuing their indie idea.

5. **Fear of success**

   Some indies are actually afraid of doing well. They can't imagine being recognized as an expert in their field. If you have fear of success, you probably believe that fame and fortune will hurt you in some way. You may think that your family and friends will like you better if you stay small.

The best way to overcome fear of success is to surround yourself with people who believe in you and who are successful themselves. Find indies or other successful people you respect and want to emulate. Spend time with people who see you as competent and capable. If you befriend successful indies you admire, it will be much easier for you to believe in and wish for your own success.

UNFORESEEN OBSTACLES

Examples of unforeseen obstacles include extreme weather conditions (blizzard, drought), technological breakdowns (computer crash, phone line damaged), and personal crises (illness, accident, robbery). (Murphy's law holds true for indies, too.)

Unforeseen obstacles can be very difficult to overcome because you have no control over them. Still, as an indie, you can take steps to overcome unforeseen obstacles by doing two things:

1. Identify the business problem which the obstacle creates.
   For example, a computer crash means that you have no access to important documents.
2. Seek assistance in solving that problem.
   The solution: Have the phone number of a computer repair person in your rolodex, and contact that person.

chapter 13
MAKING DECISIONS

Justin P. is a young business owner. His company sells and installs large steel shelves and pallet racks for warehouse storage. He needs to buy a six-wheel 18-foot box truck for hauling the racks. At first, he investigates how much a new truck would cost. The price is too high, so he decides to check out used trucks. He tells everyone he knows and scours the local papers for advertisements. The telephone rings and Justin's networking pays off. A friend of a friend is selling his truck. It's seven years old; it has 100,000 miles on it. The truck has more miles on it than Justin wants, but the price is right. What should he do?

Justin knows something about trucks and their maintenance. He'd rather buy a new truck because it would give him fewer problems, but he can't afford that now. The used truck is one-third the price; it comes from a reliable source. Justin begins to analyze his decision: Why do I need this truck? How will I use it? How important is having a truck? Can this truck help me make enough money to buy the new truck soon? Do I know someone who can help me maintain it?

After assessing the situation, Justin arrives at a decision. He'll get the highest return by buying the second-hand truck and using it to grow his business. He knows it's a little risky to buy someone else's vehicle but this immediate purchase will give his business the boost it needs. Soon, he'll be able to afford a new truck.

Decisions, Decisions, Decisions

As an indie, you'll be making all of these decisions and more.

What product or service to sell

What fees to charge

Which customer to target

What office equipment to rent/buy/borrow

What hours to work

When to make sales calls

How to make sales calls (by phone, in person)

How to bill customers or clients

How to package your product or service

To reduce his risk, Justin also decides to have his mechanic inspect the truck to make sure it is in good working condition. After his mechanic reports that the truck seems fine, Justin makes his final decision to buy it. Within 48 hours, he and the truck are on the road.

Justin's ability to weigh the pros and cons, seek professional advice, and come to a decision regarding the truck is an example of indie decision making. In Justin's case, he first decided that he needed a truck to improve his business. Next, he gathered information about the trucks available to him. Then, he assessed his options, and made a choice. Justin made an important decision for his business in a relatively short period of time. If Justin had put off his truck-buying decision, he would have stalled his business indefinitely.

Like Justin, all indies need to make good, informed decisions. The decisions you make will determine the direction your indie business will take. It's important to learn how to make good decisions within a limited period of time so that you can continue to move forward with your venture.

HOW DO YOU MAKE DECISIONS?

Part of learning how to make good decisions involves becoming familiar with your own decision-making style. Read the descriptions below, and see which "style" best describes you.

1. **Gut/intuition**—Some people go with their gut when making decisions.
   A clothing designer decides that her entire spring line should be different shades of green because she has a hunch that green will be in that season.

   Positive side of gut/intuition style: Decisions feel right and sometimes reflect hidden information in the marketplace
   Negative side of gut/intuition style: Decisions may lack important factual information

2. **Research**—Some people need to gather a lot of data before they can decide.
   A chiropractor wants to advertise his practice in a local paper. He reads every bit of information he can find about how to advertise, where to advertise, and when to advertise before he places his ad.
   Positive side of researching style: You learn a lot and make very informed decisions
   Negative side of researching style: You may become overwhelmed with information and feel unable to make a decision

3. **Emotional**—Emotional decision makers use their feelings to make all decisions. If they feel good about someone or something, they will go with it.
The owner of an organic food store hires a cashier because he "feels good" when he interviews her.

> " I made a decision several years ago not to use any sales techniques that rely on manipulation or force."
>
> Robert Agee, Sales and Management Consultant

Positive side of emotional style: Your decisions feel good in the moment
Negative side of emotional style: As your feelings change, your feelings about your decisions change

4. **Rational**—Some people rely on logic and reason when making choices. They need to know the facts and statistics concerning any topic before coming to a decision.
A computer consultant wants to buy a new printer. She thinks about her purchase, calculates her budget, and buys the printer that fits her price range and is statistically proven to perform well.

Positive side of rational style: Decisions are based on factual information and logic
Negative side of rational style: Exclusion of emotions and intuition may lead to decisions that make sense, but don't feel good over the long run

5. **Seek authority**—Authority seekers look to experts and authorities for advice before making any-decision.
A personal trainer wants to buy new weights for his gym. He contacts a professional weight lifter to find out which weights he should buy and where he should buy them.

Positive side of authority seeking: You get lots of advice from experienced experts
Negative side of authority seeking: You do not learn to develop your own opinions

6. **Nondecision**—Some people make decisions by not making them.
A budding indie artist is not sure whether he wants to submit his grant application to a major foundation for money to study overseas. He doesn't bother to get his grant application in before the deadline and becomes ineligible for the money.

Positive side of nondecision making style: You can avoid the discomfort of taking risks or making decisions.

> "I believe in recycling. I use all of my old marketing materials again. If I have a post-card or flyer that's outdated, I'll turn it over and use it for notes or phone messages."
>
> Shimoda, Jewelry Designer

"I handle data all day long—mailing lists, directories, catalogs. Whoever pays me for a job owns that information. If someone wants to buy information from me that doesn't belong to them, my decision is clearly 'no.' And the people who ask me to sell that kind of information to them are people I should probably avoid doing business with. "

David H. Jackson, Computer Services Provider

Negative side of non decision making style: Decisions will be made for you.

7. Procrastinate—This style of decision making involves delaying tactics.
The owner of an elder-care center knew she had to build a new wheel chair ramp for her senior citizens, but put off the decision to begin construction because she wasn't sure how her company would finance the project.

Positive side of procrastinating style: You buy yourself some time before making a decision
Negative side of procrastinating style: You may miss opportunities or incur penalties because you don't act fast enough

As you can see, each of these seven decision-making styles has advantages and disadvantages. The best decision makers usually combine parts of each decision making technique, and monitor their results.

With time, you'll find your own method for making good decisions. You may have some rough experiences at first because some of your decisions may turn out to be wrong. But all indies have to be willing to be wrong sometimes. Use wrong decisions for future reference. Learn from your mistakes.

Decision Making: Three Key Questions

1. **Will this decision move me towards one of my goals?**
   In our case study, Justin's decision to buy a used truck when he really wanted a new truck was a compromise, but it still moved him towards his goal. With the used truck, he knew he'd make more money and eventually buy a new truck for his business. Your business decisions should also keep you moving towards your long-range goals.

2. **Does this decision incorporate the information available to me?**
   Justin incorporated all of the information available to him before he came to his final decision. Your business decisions should also incorporate the information available to you.

3. **Does this decision agree with my ethics?**
   Your ethics are your moral principles. They are your beliefs, values, and attitudes regarding

right and wrong behavior. As an indie, it is important that your decisions agree with your ethics. You can't betray your moral code when you make a decision. For example, if you don't believe in deceiving people, then your business practices should be up front and honest. If you care about the environment, then your product or service should not harm the ecosystem. In order to make decisions that reflect your ethics, it helps to enumerate them.

> "As the owner of a graphic design company, I deal with a lot of vendors—printers, photographers, artists, production people, freelance designers, etcetera. In the process of doing a job, a lot of things can go wrong. Many designers try to hide the problems from their clients. I don't believe in deceiving my clients. If something goes wrong, I always decide to be direct and tell people what's going on. I also won't work with people who try to deceive me."
>
> Michelle Winters, Graphic Designer and Illustrator

EXPLORE YOUR ETHICS

Twenty questions to ask yourself about your indie beliefs and values

Environmental Ethics

1. Do you believe in protecting and preserving the environment?
2. Do you care if your product or service causes waste?
3. Do you care if your work pollutes the air/water/ground?
4. Are you willing to sell products or services that are hazardous to people's health?
5. Do you think recycling is important in business?
6. What actions are you willing to take to protect the environment?

People Ethics

7. Do you insist on fair treatment for yourself?
8. Do you believe in treating others fairly?
9. Do you view customers as valuable or expendable?
10. How far are you willing to go to guarantee customer satisfaction?
11. How would you respond to customer complaints?
12. When you hire someone, what rights do they have?
13. As an employer, what rights do you have?

Money Ethics

14. Do you believe in paying your bills on time?
15. Do you insist on getting paid on time?
16. Are you willing to inflate your prices to make a quick profit?
17. How much of your earnings are you willing to report to the IRS?
18. Do you think that it's okay to buy on credit?
19. Do you believe employees deserve fair wages?
20. If someone paid you twice by mistake, would you return the second payment?

"I won't do business with anyone whom I know to be dishonest."

Karen Frankfeldt, Beaded Jewelry Designer

Knowing where you stand in each of these areas will help you make good decisions.

The trick to decision making is understanding that you can't always know if you're making the right decision. Sometimes, you just have to make a decision and see where it leads you. Still, the more comfortable you become with the act of decision making, the better you'll get at it. (Remember, if you make a wrong decision, you can always make another one.)

chapter 14
TAKING RISKS

Susan B. creates handmade scarves, which she sells to boutiques in California. During the past year, she has successfully obtained ten accounts with local stores who continue to reorder every month. As positive as this sounds, the ten accounts do not generate enough income for Susan to draw a salary from her business. Susan knows that if she expanded her business and obtained ten more accounts, she could pay herself a decent salary. Unfortunately, she doesn't know how to reach the stores who'd be interested in her merchandise.

One solution to Susan's problem might be to rent a booth at a national trade show. The trade show would expose Susan to potential buyers from bou iques all over the United States. It would cost her $3,000 to participate—a hefty expense for Susan. Her booth could, however, attract the ten new accounts she needs to expand her business. While there are no guarantees that Susan would obtain new customers through the trade show, there is a good chance that she would.

Should Susan take the risk and invest $3,000 in the trade show?

Risk taking is an important skill for successful indies. Indies know that risk taking provides opportunities for growth and advancement. They live by the credo: In order to win, you must be willing to lose.

In the example above, Susan's decision regarding the trade show could result in the gain of new customers or the loss of $3,000. To a young indie, $3,000 is a lot of money. Yet, if Susan doesn't risk the investment, she loses an opportunity to meet hundreds of potential buyers.

One way to decide whether you are willing to take a risk is to list all of the possible outcomes of the risky action and see if you can live with them. In Susan's case, her investment of $3,000 to participate in the national trade show could result in one of the following:

- She could make excellent contacts at the show and obtain ten new accounts.
- She could make several good contacts at the show and obtain three or four new accounts.
- She could make many contacts at the show, but not get any immediate new business.
- The trade show could have poor attendance, and Susan may not make any good contacts.

The worst outcome in this case would involve Susan shelling out $3,000 and not meeting any new or potential customers. If Susan knows she can tolerate this worst outcome, then she can take the risk. If the worst outcome is intolerable, Susan is better off passing on the trade show.

What is your general attitude toward risk? Are you a risk avoider or risk seeker? Most people have different risk quotients for different areas of business. For example, a computer consultant may be risk seeking when it comes to sales. She may be willing to call complete strangers and ask them for business. On the other hand, she may be risk averse when it comes to financial matters. She may be unwilling to take out loans or extend her credit in any way to finance her business.

The Risk Scale

Read the following scenarios and rate yourself on the risk scale.
(1= Could never do it. 5 = Would do it immediately.)

Applying for a commercial loan

Could never do it — Would do it immediately

1 2 3 4 5

Trying out for a sports team

Could never do it — Would do it immediately

1 2 3 4 5

Auditioning for a musical group or a theatrical production

Could never do it — Would do it immediately

1 2 3 4 5

Submitting an essay you wrote for publication in a local paper

Could never do it — Would do it immediately

1 2 3 4 5

Displaying your art work at an exhibit

Could never do it				Would do it immediately
1	2	3	4	5

Running for an elected office

Could never do it				Would do it immediately
1	2	3	4	5

Asking someone you like out to a movie

Could never do it				Would do it immediately
1	2	3	4	5

Making a speech in front of your peers

Could never do it				Would do it immediately
1	2	3	4	5

Selling a product to your classmates or colleagues

Could never do it				Would do it immediately
1	2	3	4	5

RISK RATING

Add up all the numbers you picked. If you scored 33 or more, then risk taking comes easily to you. If you scored 19–32, you may be comfortable taking risks in some areas of your life, but not in others. If you scored 18 or less, you probably need to build up your risk-taking confidence.

How did you score? Were there areas in which you felt very comfortable taking risks? What were they? In the categories in which you "could never do it," are you willing to take small risks to build up you risk-taking tolerance? For example, if you are afraid to try out for a varsity or JV sports team, are you willing to try out for the intramural team instead?

Risk taking is not about taking wild chances with your money, your health, your reputation, or your safety. It is about moving out of your comfort zone and risking potential loss or failure for the sake of long-term gain. You take a risk when you do something new and you don't know what the outcome will be.

Conquering Indie Anxiety (How to Manage Entrepreneurial Fear)

Comfort

1. Join a support group.
2. Call an indie buddy on a daily or weekly basis to check in and let each other know how you are doing.
3. Engage in at least one pleasurable activity a day.
4. "Bookend" difficult activities such as cold calling or bookkeeping.

Reassurance

1. Write down every action you take towards building your business and give yourself credit for it.
2. Find people who have been through the beginning phases of becoming an indie and succeeded. Let them tell you about their early experiences.
3. Break any fear-provoking activities into smaller tasks, and coax yourself into completing one task at a time.
4. Remind yourself of past experiences when you took risks and succeeded.

Distraction

1. Go for a walk, a run, a visit with a friend.
2. Participate in a community activity that makes you feel you are making a contribution.
3. Engage yourself in some form of grounding exercise that will force you back into the present.

For indies, risk taking is a way of life. indies take risks whenever they . . .

- call potential customers
- submit proposals for freelance assignments
- invest in new office equipment
- apply for small business loans
- send out promotional materials to potential customers
- take on new projects that require high levels of expertise and professionalism.

Inevitably, there will be times when a risk taken results in failure of some kind. What indies understand is that failure is as important as success, because failure teaches valuable lessons for the future.

Sally E. was a computer consultant to small-business owners. She wanted to reach her target audience and thought that placing an ad in a local business journal would do the trick. Sally risked a $500 investment to obtain new clients. Three months passed. Sally's advertisement generated only a few calls and no concrete business. After six months, Sally still hadn't received any good leads from her ad. When she investigated the reasons for the poor return on her investment, Sally learned that her customer, the small-business owner, didn't really read the journal in which she had advertised and people tended to hire computer consultants through personal contact and referrals.

> Although Sally lost $500, her failure gave her valuable information that she could then use to devise more effective ways to get business.

As you prepare for your indie career, we encourage you to develop your ability to take prudent risks—risks that may challenge you personally but will move you toward your long-range goals.

chapter 15
MAPPING YOUR WAY TO SUCCESS

As a senior at Duke University, **Robert R.** knew what he wanted to do after graduating: open an elder care transportation service in downtown Durham. He identified the need for reliable ground transportation while volunteering at the senior citizen center near his college. Robert noticed that the seniors he befriended were often physically frail, and afraid to drive themselves to appointments and social events. He also noticed that they didn't like calling on family or friends for constant assistance. Robert wanted his elder care transportation service to shuttle senior citizens to and from their appointments. He also wanted to give seniors access to all six of the senior centers in Durham. He spent his senior year planning for Elders On The Go.

Robert set two goals for himself. First, he would write and complete his business plan in six months. Second, once the business plan was in place, he would spend another six months making all the practical arrangements for his business: Robert would raise money, rent vans, hire other drivers, and sign contracts with the Senior Centers.

With his plan on paper, Robert began to pursue his goals. He started writing his business plan in September, and completed it by the March before his graduation. During spring of his senior year, Robert began pulling together all the practical details of his business—he found investors, raised $10,000, leased four vans, hired four drivers, and signed contracts with all six of Durham's Senior Centers.

The September after Robert graduated, his transportation service was up and running. The year he'd spent planning and taking successive steps to launch his business allowed him to open Elders On The Go on the target date.

Vague Goal	Clear Goal
Plan my business	Write a business plan
Make money	Make $500 per month
Sell sports equipment	Sell 30 mitts, 50 baseballs, 10 bats
Obtain tutoring work	Obtain six students to tutor weekly at $40 per hour
Advertise my housecleaning business	Advertise my housecleaning business by placing three ads in local paper and posting 100 flyers

Goal setting and planning are at the root of any successful indie business. Learning how to plan effectively and map out the steps to achieving your goals may take time and practice. Nevertheless, the ability to set goals and plan for long-term results is crucial for anyone who wants to bring an indie idea into reality. Without a plan, most indies don't get where they want to go.

YOUR INDIE ROAD MAP

You wouldn't get into your car and drive across the country without a map, would you? (If so, your trip would be a long one!) Goal setting and planning give you a map to follow, a direction towards which you can steer your efforts.

Clear Goals Get You There Faster

When setting goals, it's important to remember that goals should be specific and measurable. The more concrete your goals are the easier it will be for you to reach them. If they're too vague, you won't be able to gauge your success. For instance, Robert's goal to write a business plan in six months was specific and measurable.

At the end of six months, Robert would know whether he'd completed a written business plan for Elders On The Go. If he'd written three-quarters of it, he could say that he reached 75 percent of his goal. If Robert had set a general or vague goal ("I want to plan my business"), he'd have more difficulty measuring his success. Effective goals are clear and recognizable. You know when you accomplish them.

The more specific and measurable your goals are, the more likely you are to attain exactly what you want. After you have written a goal, ask yourself, "Will I be able to recognize this if I reach it?" If the answer is yes, you are on the right track.

Set Goals Four Times a Year

It is standard practice to set goals four times a year. These quarterly goals should be written at the start of every new season. Three-month goals are easy to follow. When the quarter is over, you can calculate what percent of your goals you've achieved and determine how much further you have to go.

Sample Quarterly Goals

Date: **January 1**
Name: **Mark Print**
Business/Profession: **Desktop publisher**
Major Goals: (Be specific and measurable within a twelve week period)

1. **Write the marketing section of my business plan by 3/30**
2. **Obtain two new clients that generate $1,000 per month by 3/30**
3. **Set up bookkeeping system and record all expenses and income for last three months by 2/15**
4. **Find two new places to speak about my services by 3/30**

Write Your Goals Down

Indies always write their goals down on paper. Indies know that putting goals in print increases the likelihood of achieving them. Once you write goals down, it also helps to read them twice a day. Reading your goals two times a day will keep them in the forefront of your mind.

> The mind moves towards whatever is in front of it. Put your goals in front.

Four to Five Goals Are Best

It's best not to have too many goals at one time. If you try to achieve too many things at once, you may become overwhelmed and confused. Limit yourself to four or five goals per quarter.

> Too many goals may overwhelm you. Five solid goals are enough.

From Goals To Tasks

Goals give you the Big Picture. Once you set goals, the next step is to list specific actions you'll take to accomplish each goal. We call these specific actions "tasks." Charting the tasks involved with reaching each goal gives you a concrete plan of action.

Name	Lottie Suds
Business	Spic and Span Dog-Washing Boutique
Goal	To have my dog-washing business increase by $500 per month (15 new customers at $15.00 per wash)
Tasks	Put ad in local newspaper
	Send out 300 flyers to neighborhood dog owners
	Make 30 follow-up phone calls per week
	Meet with 3 veterinarians and ask for referrals
	Go to local park once a week and hand out business cards to dog owners
	Attend Spring Dog Show and pass out flyers
	Establish referral system with local dog walkers

As Lottie's example illustrates, tasks spell out the actions you'll take to produce your desired outcome. Every time you complete a task, you move one step closer to achieving your goal.

SCHEDULING FOR RESULTS

The final phase of goal setting involves writing down when you plan to work on your tasks. We recommend blocking out time in your calendar so that you know when to work on each task. This step is called scheduling for results. It's an extremely important habit for indies to cultivate. We find that indies who don't block out the time to do their tasks often get sidetracked.

May P. wanted to write an article for her college's quarterly magazine. She had three months to write her piece, and she felt no pressure to complete it. She thought she would work on it one evening a week. May didn't designate a particular evening when she had to write, nor did she block out the time physically in her calendar. As each week passed, May constantly told herself that she would work on the article "tomorrow evening." If a friend called and asked her out to a movie, May always said yes. Two weeks before the article was due, May panicked. She hadn't even written a rough draft. For the next 13 days, May forced herself to work on the magazine article night and day. By the time she handed her piece to the editor, she was exhausted. "If I had just blocked out one evening a week in my calendar, I could have written this article without killing myself."

When you reserve time to work on your tasks, finding the time to complete them is not a problem.

Goal Setting Takes Practice

Goal setting is a skill which takes time to develop. When you first set your goals, several things can happen:

1. **You may achieve your goals.**

   In this case, you can congratulate yourself and prepare your next set of goals.

2. **You may find out that the goals you set were wrong for you.**

   As you pursue your goals, you may realize that they aren't really the right goals for you. For example: You may think you want a food catering business, but as you begin to get catering jobs, you realize you don't really like preparing food all the time and you don't like managing food servers. Discovering that you don't want a certain goal is good because it will bring you closer to understanding what you really do want. If the first set of goals you set turn out to be wrong for you, you can set new ones. (Being an indie involves a lot of trial and error.)

3. **You may have to back up and accomplish preliminary goals before you can accomplish your original goals.**

   Sometimes a goal you set may wind up requiring a whole set of preliminary goals before you can pursue it. For example, you may want to sell your services as a personal trainer. The only problem is that, as you research your idea, you find out that you have to be certified as an aerobics instructor before you can be insured for possible injury to your clients. In that case, you'll have to undergo training and obtain certification (preliminary goals) before you can hire out as a trainer (original goal).

4. **You may underestimate the time it takes to accomplish your goals.**

   This outcome is very common among new indies. Until you've had some experience setting quarterly goals and tracking your progress, you won't know how long it actually takes to accomplish certain things. For example, if you decide to make a brochure describing your business, it may take much longer than you estimate to write the copy, design the layout, find a printer, and produce the final brochure. You may think you can do it in four weeks when it actually takes four months.

One of the major benefits of quarterly goal setting is that it shows you what you are capable of achieving in a given time frame. Once you have charted your goals for four quarters, you can go back and assess your performance. Your second year of setting goals will be much more accurate in terms of time estimates.

With time and practice, you'll learn how to map out your goals and tasks effectively. You'll also experience great satisfaction in making them happen.

chapter 16
MARKETING

During her senior year of high school, **Carol K.** began tutoring young teens in computer skills. She taught kids ages 12 and up how to use computers for writing reports, making charts, and surfing the Internet for information. Carol charged her students $20 per hour—a fee most parents were happy to pay. She liked making the extra money and she loved working with kids. When Carol went to college, she missed the money from tutoring, and decided to start selling her service again. The only problem was that Carol was in a new town where she didn't know the locals.

At home, her students were junior high school kids from her neighborhood. Carol knew most of the parents, and business just came to her. Now, she needed to find new potential students, and convince their parents to hire her. The challenge of finding new business in foreign territory sent Carol to her college library, where she digested a book on marketing.

The ideas presented in that book opened Carol's mind to new ways of thinking. Carol realized that, in order to reach her customers (parents and their young teenage kids), she needed to go to the places where they hang out. Carol decided to post fliers on bulletin boards all over town—in local grocery stores, Laundromats, family restaurants, and libraries. She called the town's junior high schools and offered free lectures to students on using the Internet. She went to the local computer store and asked if they would give out her business cards to parents in search of computer instruction for their kids. On Saturdays, Carol stood on the busiest corner of town and passed out her fliers to families as they walked by. Within one month, Carol acquired six students who saw her weekly for computer lessons. Her marketing had really paid off.

Marketing is any action you take to bring your product or service to your customer's attention. Marketing is an umbrella term covering several different activities: advertising, public relations, direct mail, networking, and promotions.

The purpose of marketing is to generate sales. In the example above, every action Carol took—from posting fliers to contacting schools—brought her tutoring service to the attention of potential customers. If she hadn't taken those steps, no one would've known about her.

Effective marketing is the single most important skill you'll need for indie success. Marketing is essential because it generates "leads," that is potential customers. Once you have leads, you can convert them into paying customers. Without leads, you don't have any potential business. It's that simple. Smart indies know that marketing deserves their time and attention. They learn how to use it to their indie advantage.

SAMPLE CUSTOMER PROFILE

Business: Carol K.'s Computer Tutoring Service

Age: School kids, ages 12–15 (their parents actually pay for the service)

Gender: Girls and boys

Income: Parents need to make $35,000 and up to pay for my service.

Geographic Location: Within five miles of my college dormitory (can travel to customer's home via bicycle and/or public transportation)

SAMPLE CUSTOMER BEHAVIOR PROFILE

Business: Carol K.'s Computer Tutoring Service

Customer: Students ages 12–16 and their parents.

Customer Interests: Sports, social clubs, art, music

Customer's activities: Play sports, cheerlead, participate in performing arts (drama, dance, chorus), draw, and paint

Shopping Habits: Go to local mall, Visit stores on Main Street

Reading Habits: *Daily Herald* newspaper, neighborhood newsletters

Other Places Where My Customers Get Information: Local bulletins boards, public library, online services, school teachers and counselors, other students and parents

DEFINING YOUR CUSTOMER

Before you decide on the type of marketing you want to do, you need to identify your customer—the person or group who might buy your product or service. Your customer cannot be everyone. For example, Carol's customers were students (ages 12–16) and their parents. Carol pinpointed this group because the kids needed computer skills for school, and the parents were eager to enhance their children's capabilities.

Once you have an indie product or service, think of who would want to buy it. Describe exactly who your customer is. What is your customer's age? What is your customer's gender? Are you selling to men, women, girls, boys, all of the above? How much money does your customer make? Define your customer's geographic parameters. Is your customer located in your neighborhood, your town, your state? Do your customers come to you or do you go to them?

Next, consider your customer's behavior patterns: Where do they get their information? What are your customer's interests and activities? Where does this population shop? What do your customers read? How would you catch this audience's attention? The more clearly you can answer these questions, the easier it will be to find potential buyers. Once you've defined your customer, you can devise a marketing strategy for getting their attention.

MARKETING STRATEGIES

There are several marketing strategies which indies use to heighten customer interest and awareness.

Advertising

Advertising encompasses any message in print, film, or tape that encourages your customer to buy your product. Advertising space can be bought from newspapers, newsletters, catalogues, online services. Advertising includes listings in The Yellow Pages, billboard displays, T.V., and radio commercials.

For Carol K., the fliers she posted all over town were her version of advertising. Carol's fliers alerted students and parents about her computer tutoring service and gave them a phone number to call for an initial consultation. Carol lacked the funds to buy ad space in the local newspaper, so she figured out where her potential customers would go—supermarkets, libraries, laundromats, etcetera—and posted her printed message there.

Advertising is often the first marketing method new. Indies employ to attract potential customers. Unfortunately, expensive advertising is not always very effective. Advertising space can be very costly and yield few results. Most customers need to see an ad six times before they actually consider buying.

If you decide to advertise your indie business, aim for repetition and consistency. Be willing to say the same message over and over again. Remember that small ads seen many times by your potential customer will yield better results than one large ad seen once.

Public Relations (P.R.)

Public Relations involves marketing activities that promote a favorable relationship with the public. Free lectures, radio or T.V. interviews, printed articles, press conferences, involvement in community events all go under the heading of public relations.

In the example above, Carol gave free lectures to students about surfing the Net. This public service gave Carol excellent exposure as a computer expert. Because she offered her lectures in junior high schools, she was sure to find potential customers among her audience members.

Public relations is a favorite marketing activity for many indies. Used correctly, it can serve as free advertising. You can write press releases about your company and send them to local publications. You can write articles that educate your customer and get them published. You can be interviewed as an expert in your industry on a radio show or T.V. show. P.R. includes participating in community events and/or donating your product or services to a special cause. All of these actions give indies exposure and credibility.

Direct Mail

Direct Mail is any mail piece intended to sell a product or service. Postcards, brochures, catalogues, letters, fliers, and coupons are all direct mail pieces. Anything designed to sell something that goes through the mail is considered direct mail.

Direct mail usually plays an important role in any indie's marketing campaign. Whether it's a brochure, a catalog, a postcard, or a letter, direct mail can send a message to many people about your product or service. For example, Carol K. could produce a postcard describing her computer tutoring service. She could send this mail piece to every family in town with kids enrolled in junior high school.

You can spend very little on direct mail (postcard) or you can spend a lot (catalogs). Whatever the cost, your first challenge is to design a mail piece that your customer will read. (How may times do you throw away mail because you know someone is selling you something?) In other words, indie mail pieces need to be interesting and appealing. Avoid sending out anything looking like junk mail.

Networking

Networking is the act of making connections with people who may bring you new business. You are networking whenever you go to places, events, social functions, conferences, or trade shows where you might meet potential customers.

In Carol K.'s example, she practiced two different networking techniques:

- She gave her business cards to computer stores so that they could refer potential customers to her
- She stood on the street corner and introduced herself to parents and their kids while handing out her fliers

Networking is a necessary element for generating indie business opportunities. People like to do business with people they know. Going out and meeting people who are your potential customers is an inexpensive marketing avenue that has big return. Smart indies go to places where they'll meet potential clients on an ongoing basis. For example, Paul G., a photographer, attends meeting at the local chapter of the National Speaker's Association. He goes there because he knows that he will meet public speakers who need headshots.

A common mistake that new indies make is going to events where they meet their peers expecting to find new business. Paul G. could spend his time attending meetings at photographers' associations. While he may learn new technical things about his industry, he most probably will not meet potential customers. Going to the Speaker's Association is more conducive to meeting customers.

Another common mistake in networking involves how indies attend an event. If you enter a room and don't talk to anyone, you are not networking. Smart indies set networking goals like, "I will hand out no fewer than ten business cards at this event," and " I can't leave until I receive ten business cards."

Promotions

Promotions are products that you give potential customers to encourage them to buy from you. Promotions include free gifts, free samples, gift certificates, free publications, and discounts.

Promotions are a way of allowing your customer to experience your product or service at no cost to them.

Sample promotions:

A hair salon offers the first haircut at 50 percent off.
A software company gives a 30-day trial period.
A new bakery hands out homemade cookies on the street.

You've probably had the experience of getting free shampoo in the mail. Did you use it? Did you buy it afterwards? Sometimes promotions work and sometimes they don't.

If Carol K. wanted to attract more tutoring students, she could offer a half hour of free computer instruction. Promotions can be effective because people are more likely to buy something they have already tried. The trick to promotions is knowing that, while nine out of ten people may take your promotion, they won't all become your customers. Promotions enlarge your customer potential.

As an indie, you'll need to decide which marketing tactics you want to use to reach your customer. It's always better to use a combination of efforts rather than relying on any single activity. For instance, Carol put fliers up in different locations (advertising), gave her business cards to the computer store (networking), and offered free lectures to students (public relations). Carol's willingness to try a variety of marketing techniques gave her excellent exposure—a key element in effective marketing.

The purpose of marketing is customer awareness. These methods make your customer aware that your product/service exists. The next step is selling, which we'll discuss in the next chapter.

chapter 17
SALES

Kay S., a personal chef, was out shopping one Monday morning for a client. She filled her basket with ten different vegetables and five different fresh fruits. While Kay was standing in the checkout line, the woman behind her asked, "What are you going to make with that assortment?" Kay explained that she cooked for families as a profession, and this was the food she would be preparing for one of her customers.

The woman became very interested in Kay's personal chef service. She introduced herself: "My name is Briana. I'm the mother of three, and I'm sick and tired of preparing dinner every night for my family." Briana asked for more information about Kay's service. Kay described her system: She went into her customers' home on a weekday and cooked seven dinners for the week. The first two were refrigerated and the other five were frozen; all dishes were labeled with the ingredients, number of calories, and directions for heating.

Briana couldn't believe it. She got excited at the thought of someone doing all of the shopping and cooking for her family dinners. She asked Kay for her phone number and what the cost of her service would be. When Kay told her the cost, Briana said it was very reasonable. Kay gave Briana her business card. She also took down Briana's phone number and set up a telephone appointment for later that day.

Later that day, Kay sat down to make sales calls to potential clients. Her first call was to Briana. Kay knew that Briana was a hot lead. Briana sounded harried on the phone. "I don't have much time to talk," she said. Kay understood Briana's situation—feeling rushed and overwhelmed was a key reason people hired Kay to do their cooking. So, Kay took the "too busy" cue and went into her sale:

Kay: Briana, you sound so overwhelmed. No wonder you're interested in my service.
Briana: Yes I am. Tell me about it quickly.

Kay: Briana, does grocery shopping and preparing dinner give you stress in your life that you could do without?
Briana: Yes it does.

Kay: And do you think that if I took all of that off your hands you'd have more time and feel less stress?
Briana: Yes I would.

Kay: Then why don't we try one week and see how your family likes it?
Briana: All right, let's try a week.

Kay: Let me come over tomorrow at 8:00 A.M. How is that?
Briana: For what?

Kay: So that you can pick out your menu.
Briana: I don't have time tomorrow.

Kay: I understand. Why don't I fax over the menu now? Let's pick out your meals, and you can pay by credit card so you don't have to waste time sending me a check.
Briana: O.K. Let's do it now.

And with that, Kay completed the sale.

The ability to sell is essential for your success as an indie. In the previous chapter, we examined marketing and talked about the many activities you can do to bring in potential customers—advertising, P.R., direct mail, and promotions, etcetera. Sales converts potential customers into paying customers. You need to know how to sell so that people actually buy your product or service, and you can make money.

Indies use selling skills for . . .

- Winning freelance, part-time and/or temporary jobs
- Contacting potential customers and getting appointments to meet with them
- Selling their services to companies, individuals, groups
- Selling their products to retailers, wholesalers, individuals
- Selling new products or services to existing customers

Most people envision sales as an artificial process where they have to manipulate or push someone into buying something from them. Smart indies know that effective sales is as natural as a good conversation. As Kay's story illustrates, you can find out what your customer wants, let them know how you can help, and close a sale with ease. The key to effective selling is learning how to ask the right questions so that you can uncover what your potential customer really needs.

Understand What Your Customer is Buying

In order to ask potential customers the right questions, you must understand what they are buying from you. That means you need to know why your customer would want your product or service in the first place. People buy value. That is, we don't buy matches, we buy fire. We don't buy umbrellas, we buy protection from the rain.

What is the value of your product or service? What is your customer really buying from you? Indies need to distinguish between the characteristics of what they are selling (concrete features of their product/service) and the value of what they are selling (benefit to the customer).

People buy value. We don't buy matches, we buy fire. We don't buy umbrellas, we buy protection from the rain.

Business: Personal Chef

Characteristic	Value
Home-cooked meals for one week	• Good tasting, nutritional food • Relief from cooking • More time for other things • Food that tastes better than takeout

---

Business: Dog walking	
Characteristic	**Value**
Show up at 1:00 P.M. every day to walk dog	• Dog has regular companionship • Dog is less lonely • Dog gets exercise • Owner feels less guilty about leaving dog at home

Business: Interior Decorating	
Characteristic	**Value**
Go into home. Come up with personalized, tasteful design plan	• Save customer time and effort • Elevate customer's image • Give customer's home unified, balanced look

Business: Computer Tutor	
Characteristic	**Value**
Teach teenagers computer skills	• Teenager masters different computer programs • Teenager receives good adult supervision • Teenager becomes more interested in school subjects

While it's important to describe the characteristics of your indie business, the value is what customers buy. And value differs from person to person. What's valuable to one customer may not be valuable to another. It's your job to discover what each potential customer considers valuable.

In Kay's example, Briana wanted relief from the stress of preparing dinner every night for her family ("I am sick and tired of preparing dinner every night for my family".) While Kay may think she's selling nutritious and tasty food, she's really selling convenience and less stress. For customers like Briana, nutrition and good taste are secondary to the relief she'll experience because someone else is cooking dinner. During her next sales call, Kay may talk to a potential customer who has different needs from Briana. For example, she might talk to a busy executive who has no time to cook and is sick of takeout meals. In that case, homemade food and relaxing meals are what the customer is buying.

Ask People What They Need

As we've already mentioned, the key to effective selling is learning how to ask the right questions so that you can uncover what your potential customer really needs. Asking questions brings out important information. You learn your customers' opinions and values. Questions are interactive so the customer must listen in order to respond.

Let's look at Kay's call to Briana. Once Kay got Briana on the phone, she asked two questions: "Does shopping and preparing dinner take more time out of your day than you'd like?" and "Do you think that if I took all of that off your hands you'd feel less stress?" Kay knew that Briana was interested in her service, and her questions showed that she understood Briana's need for more time and less stress. When Briana answered yes to both of those questions, Kay could move on with the sale.

SALES PRESCRIPTION

These five steps help you know what actions to take while you're making a sale:

1. Ask people what they need.
2. Give them what they need.
3. Ask for the business.
4. Field a "no."
5. Get a "yes."

Now, if another potential customer were interested in a personal chef service for nutrition purposes, Kay would follow a different line of questioning. She could ask, "How important is low-fat, healthy cooking to you and your family?" If the answer was, "It's very important," Kay could continue down that road of questions. Example: "How would you like to be able to provide your family with seven delicious, nutritious meals a week without laboring over the stove yourself?"

There's a saying in sales: "If you're telling you aren't selling." Kay could have called Briana and just talked at her, telling Briana how great her personal chef service was, hoping Briana would buy. Instead, Kay asked two important questions and got Briana involved in the sale. If you ask your potential customers thoughtful questions based on what you're selling, it will help them understand why they need your product or service.

Give Them What They Need

Once you find out what your potential customers need, you can give them what they need through your words and actions. For example, Kay understood that Briana was stressed out and short on time. She eliminated any meetings by faxing Briana her menus and letting Briana pay for the service via credit card. If Kay were selling a nutrition-oriented customer, she could go over the nutrients in each dish, and discuss which meals would be best for her family's dietary considerations.

Giving your customers what they need may involve demonstrating your product or service, or explaining how you can solve the customer's problem. It always involves responding to the customer's concerns. Kay understood that Briana was stressed out and short on time. For example, Kay knows that most of her clients buy her service to obtain more time, so she has found ways to make buying her service easy and fast.

Ask for the Business

Once you understand what a potential customer needs and you demonstrate how your product or service can fulfill that need, then it's time to *ask for the business*. Customers need to be asked because they usually don't buy until someone brings the sale to a close. Asking for the business can be done in many ways. You can say, "How would you like to pay for that?" or, "If you sign here, we can begin Monday." These statements are called *closes*. One of two things can happen when you close. Your potential customer can say "yes," and you've got new business. Or he/she can say "no" and you've got some more work ahead of you.

Fielding a "No"

When a potential customer says no, it's not always a bad sign. Most of the time, it really means, "I am not sold yet," or "I don't have enough information," or "You haven't uncovered my real need." Never take no as a get-lost-go-away-no. Always counter a no with a "why?" Your job is to field the "no" by finding out more about the customer. For instance, if Briana told Kay, "No, call me in a week," Kay could have gone back to questioning Briana:

Kay: How will you prepare dinner for your family next week?
Brian: We will be out of town next week.

Kay: O.K., then why don't we consider the following week and sign up now?
Briana: O.K. Let's do it.

"No" may mean "not now," but don't run away from it. Embrace it and see what's underneath.

Getting a "Yes"

When customers are ready to buy they often give buying signals:

(In person)
- Move closer to you physically because they're feeling good about you and their decision
- Breathe a sigh of relief because they have made a decision
- Start talking faster because they are ready to complete the transaction

(On the telephone)
- Become more chatty and relaxed because they have made a decision
- Become impatient because they are ready to complete
- Start closing the sale themselves by asking where to send the check

When you sense a buying signal, it's time to ask for the business. If you get a "yes," always follow it up with a concrete action that will solidify the customer's commitment. Concrete actions include securing a nonrefundable deposit, or obtaining a signed sales contract or an order form. (Signed documents create a stronger commitment than a verbal "yes.")

Sales is a numbers game. The more people you try to sell, the more success you'll have. While it may be tough to ask for the business and risk hearing "no" from a potential customer, it's important to assume that you will get a "yes" eventually. If they really need what you're offering and they can afford it, most potential customers will probably become paying customers sooner or later.

People Buy Differently

When selling, remember you are asking people to do two difficult things: Make a decision, and spend money. These two challenges evoke different buying styles in different people. Check the two buying that most likely refer to the way you shop. One for small personal purchases (clothes, haircuts) and one for big-ticket items and investments (car, school).

Boutique of Buyers—12 Buying Styles

Style	Behavior
Egos	Need to acquire the newest, best, and biggest because it makes them feel important.
Hesitaters	Procrastinate, take a long time to decide. Puts off decisions as long as possible.
Feelers	Buying is emotional. If it feels good they buy. If it feels bad, they don't.
Spontaniacs	Act without thought. Get a rush from the excitement of buying.
Doubters	Disbelieve at first, then sometimes come around with enough information.
Eternal Returners	Ambivalent about everything. Need help in making a decision and staying with it.
Reasoners	Only buy when they really need something. Rational reasoning, usually buy when it's profitable.
Easy Prey	Can't say "no"; say they will buy; hide instead of saying "no."
Discount Demons	Always need to feel that they're getting a deal.
Packaging Pushovers	Buy the packaging. Equate beauty with quality.
Investigators	Does a lot of research before buying. Needs time to check things out. Look for by degrees, referrals, and so on.
Compulsives	Buy uncontrollably, spend too much, can't pay bills.

Bye-Bye Buyer . . .

A Doubter trying to sell a Compulsive may talk that person out of buying by flooding him or her with unnecessary information. A Feeler selling a Reasoner may lose a potential customer by focusing on feelings rather than facts. A Spontaniac trying to sell an Investigator may infuriate the buyer. The Spontaniac wants the Investigator to buy quickly, while the Investigator has a lot of questions.

Indies know that when they make a sale, they tend to project their own buying styles onto the customer. For instance, if you're a Procrastinator, you may take a long time to buy. You may give up on a customer who's ready to buy because you assume he or she buys the way you do. We tend to sell the way we buy because it's the way we want to be sold.

You may have several purchasing styles depending on the scale of the purchase. Identify your buying style and suspend it while you're selling.

Type of Indie Work	% of Time Spent Selling	What You Are Selling	Whom You're Selling To
Temp	20%	your skills	temp agencies
Freelancer	40%	your service	clients/companies
Consultant	60%	your expertise and advice	clients/companies
Business Owner	80%	your product or service	customers

Learning how to sell is one of the most valuable skills any indie can master. It takes persistence and consistency. The challenge in selling is separating yourself personally from the "nos" and seeing that the rejection is not about you. There will always be "no's," since you cannot sell everyone. Successful indies see that a "no" brings them one step closer to the next "yes."

chapter 18
FLEXIBILITY

Everyone was on the set. The actors, the technicians, the writers, the crew, and the client. Three hours into production, the client approached his producer, **Doug W.** "I'm afraid this shoot is going badly. This video is not what I had in mind." Even though he'd already approved the script and understood what Doug was trying to achieve, the client insisted that the current product was not what he wanted.

Doug, without missing a beat, asked the filming crew to take a break. He then held an impromptu meeting with the actors, writers, and client. He asked the client to voice his opinion to everyone. While the client explained his misgivings about what he'd seen on the set, Doug and the writers began to rewrite and recompose the video.

Within two hours, the video had taken on a new life. The client was pleased with the revised script and staging. Because everyone on the set was flexible, they were able to adjust to the new production goals, and go back to work with ease.

To practice flexibility requires a willingness to respond to immediate events without judgment or rigidity. Doug W.'s situation with the unhappy client could have turned out differently. If Doug hadn't been willing to shift gears to suit his client, he and his crew could have lost the job altogether. Instead, Doug responded to his client's feedback, and revised the video even as they were filming it. Doug W. created a flexible environment in which everyone flowed with the change.

Savvy indies are able to go with the flow, be creative and respond to their immediate circumstances. They're open to suggestion and don't assume that they have all the answers.

"Responding to circumstances"; "Spontaneous creativity"; "Not having the answers"; "Going with the flow".

These are not words that carry weight in the corporate world. In fact, these ideas are a threat to the foundation of a stable, predictable corporate environment. But to aspiring indies enterprise, these terms are a way of life. As the rapidly changing marketplace continues to challenge us to update our skills and products, it will also challenge us to adapt quickly to changing circumstances.

BENDING THE RULES, NOT BREAKING THEM

Flexibility involves bending your own rules, but not breaking them. It means going with the flow without being a doormat. There are times when it's good to be flexible, and times when you should not be. Appropriate flexibility requires good personal judgment. You have to ask yourself if it will help you in the long run to be flexible in the moment.

Ava S., a graphic designer, had a particular client, a small cosmetics company, for whom she designed all the packaging. She'd been working with this client for three years. They always paid on time, and they always treated her with respect. One day, the head of marketing approached Ava and informed her that the company was experiencing some short-term financial difficulties. He asked Ava if she could design the next set of packages at a discounted rate. He emphasized that this was an usual situation, and that they would not make this kind of request on a regular basis. Ava considered the situation and decided that she was willing to reduce her fee for this particular project.

In this example, Ava used her personal judgment to decide whether she was willing to reduce her fee for a long-standing client. She agreed to take on the project at a discounted rate because she wanted to preserve her relationship with the company, and because she wanted to keep the door open for future business. If this same client approached Ava again requesting another discounted fee, she might reassess the situation and come to a different decision.

Allan G., an accountant, had a client who kept scheduling appointments with him only to call and cancel one hour before the meeting. Allan wanted to be flexible, but he got the distinct feeling that this particular client was jerking him around. After the third cancellation, Allan decided to set down some rules. He said that the next appointment would cost $75—even if the client canceled. While Allan normally liked being flexible, he believed that this situation warranted a stricter policy.

DEVELOPING YOUR FLEXIBILITY STYLE

Your ideas about flexibility will shape and influence your indie business. You can decide in what ways you're willing to be flexible, and in what ways you won't bend. Here are some ways in which your flexibility will be tested.

Adjusting the Design of Your Product or Service

Sometimes, a potential client or customer wants what you have to offer—with slight modifications. Smart indies are willing to be flexible about the design of their product or service as long as it doesn't hurt the quality of their business.

> You're a sales trainer who normally gives two-hour seminars.
> A major corporation wants to hire you, but only wants a one-hour presentation. You redesign your seminar to fit into that time frame.

Adjusting to Clients' Time Constraints

The information age has made time an extremely valuable commodity. Many potential customers are very busy and need you to be flexible enough to adjust to their time constraints.

> You're a personal trainer, and you get a call from one of your clients. The client can't make her regular appointment because she must attend an important business meeting. You adapt to this situation and reschedule to meet later in the week.

Adjusting to Changes in Your Industry

Smart indies keep abreast of the trends in their industry and make conscious decisions about how they will adapt to the significant changes that affect their product or service.

> You're a professional photographer and you notice that many of your competitors use Web pages to display and sell their photographs. You are willing to adjust to this new development and invest in your own Web page.

Changing Your Work Environment

Mobile and interchangeable work environments are increasingly the norm these days. Indies understand that flexibility in this area increases their chances for success.

> You're a freelance copywriter. Client A wants you to work on the company premises while client B prefers that you work off-site, at your own office. You adapt to both requests by going to client A two days a week, and working for client B at home.

Practicing flexibility in any of these areas could provide you with more opportunities and more business than taking a rigid stance. Of course, there are also areas in which you should not be flexible. These include:

Compromising or Betraying Your Ethics and Values

Because your business reputation will depend upon your business practices, you don't want to do things that compromise your ethics and values.

> You design and sell computer software programs and you're negotiating with the chief buyer of a large corporation. The buyer tells you that he'll give you a larger order if you pay him money under the table.

Allowing Yourself to Be Hired By Someone Without Securing a Written Agreement Spelling Out the Terms of Your Relationship

Written contracts or letters of agreement are extremely important in any indie business transaction. They give you the concrete backup you need to receive the treatment and payment for which you bargained.

> You are a freelancer package designer and a new client needs packages designed in a rush. They claim that there is no need for a written contract, that it would take too long to write it up. You decide to believe them. Six months later, you're still chasing after the money they owe you for the job.

Slicing Your Fees So That You Can't Make a Profit

While it may be prudent to offer certain customers or clients discounts sometimes, there is a point at which your indie business will suffer if you continually slice your prices.

> You make fine jewelry and a high-profile department store expresses interest in selling your goods. They are willing to pay only 50 percent of your wholesale price. If you sell your jewelry at that price, you will actually lose money.

ADVANCED STRATEGIES: THE BUSINESS OF BOUNDARIES

Interpersonal boundaries are invisible lines we draw between ourselves and the people in our lives. They define the limits of our relationships. In business, boundaries are extremely important because they spell out acceptable and unacceptable behavior.

Let's say a customer calls you at home at 11:00 P.M. *Boundary Question: Do you take the call or ask them to call you tomorrow during regular business hours?*

Indies constantly face situations where they must communicate their interpersonal boundaries to customers and staff. You set a boundary every time you . . .

- Establish the terms of payment between yourself and a client
- Decide how much time you will give a prospective customer free of charge
- Describe the kind of behavior you expect from your hired help
- Set clear policies about doing business with friends
- Limit the hours during which you receive business calls
- Reserve specific days for relaxation and social activities

Boundary Basics

1. Interpersonal boundaries are invisible. They have to be communicated in order to be known.
2. Effective business boundaries are conveyed through consistent words and actions. (Mixed messages yield mixed results.)
3. If there is an area of your business which causes you feelings of anger or confusion, you probably need to set a boundary.

Boundary Tips

One way to strengthen your business boundaries is to write them down. Price lists, payment policies, client agreements and staff requirements are much easier to enforce when they're on paper.

When you set a boundary, be prepared to follow through with it. People naturally want to test each other's limits. Any boundary you establish will probably be tested.

Pursue business relationships with people who respect your boundaries. Let go of people who treat you poorly or constantly cross your acceptable behavior line.

chapter 19

FINANCIAL PLANNING

Joseph D. started his technical writing business on a shoestring. He had $1,800 in the bank and one new client who would be paying him $1,000 a month for six months. He worked out of his home, so he had no office rent to pay, and he already owned a computer. With such low start-up costs, Joseph could begin his indie business with a minimum outlay of funds.

Joseph calculated his personal living expenses for one month. He estimated that the amount of money he needed to cover his rent, telephone, food, gas, and car payments was approximately $800. Because he had a cash reserve of $1,800, Joseph thought he'd be okay. By the end of the first month, he'd receive the first $1,000 payment from his new client and everything would be smooth sailing from there—or so he thought.

Joseph was missing some key information when he made his calculations. First, Joseph forgot about estimated taxes. He didn't realize that, out of every dollar he made as an indie, he needed to set aside 20 cents for quarterly tax payments that were due every three months. Suddenly, Joseph's $1,000 a month income was reduced to $800.

Second, Joseph didn't know that he'd be paid 30 days *after* billing the client. This meant that Joseph wouldn't see any money for a full two months after he started working. This lag forced him to use $1,600 of his $1,800 "reserve money" for two months of living expenses.

Third, in order to generate more clients, Joseph had to spend some money on marketing materials. He needed business cards to hand out at networking events, and a mail piece to send to prospective customers. He needed envelopes, stationery, and postage for basic correspondence. Joseph's marketing costs added another $75 per month to his expenses.

Joseph's first six months as an indie were very tight financially. Because he earned $725 per month after expenses (marketing materials and taxes), he had to watch every penny and keep his personal spending down to the bare bones. Also, even when he obtained new clients, he couldn't expect payment for the work he did for at least 30 days.

In retrospect, Joseph sees how he underestimated the financial aspects of opening a business: "I should have taken more time to research and plan out the money side of my business. Then it wouldn't have been so stressful during my first year of operations."

Still, the nerve-wracking experience of "just getting by" taught Joseph some valuable lessons. During his second year of business, he took a small-business financial management course. He learned basic bookkeeping skills. He also learned how to make sales projections and how to manage the flow of cash in his business. With a little practice, Joseph discovered simple ways to budget for the ups, downs, delays, and unexpected expenses that are a normal part of self-employment.

The ultimate reality of any business is its ability to make money. For indies, making money is a twofold process. First, there is the money the business makes. In Joseph's case, his business brought in gross sales of $1,000 per month for the first six months.

$1,000 per month = Gross Sales

Second, there's the money your business nets, that is, the money you have after expenses.

Gross sales – Operating Expenses = Business Net Income

Joseph's monthly expenses included his marketing materials ($75) and his taxes ($200).

$1000 – $275 = $725 (net income)

Joseph's indie venture was a *service business:* He sold his expertise as a writer. He ran his business from his home, using equipment he already owned. So Joseph's initial expenses (also called "start-up costs") were extremely low.

But there were other factors that affected the flow of cash in his business. For Joseph, setting aside money for taxes, spending money on marketing materials, and waiting 30 days for payment were unexpected financial factors that put him on a monetary tightrope for the first six months of his indie career.

> "Probably the most common error people make during the startup period is to anticipate cash revenues sooner than they should. The general rule: Cash will come in more slowly and go out more rapidly than you expect."
>
> David H. Bangs, Jr.

Careful financial planning and consistent financial record keeping are two extremely important practices to cultivate when you're running a business. Before you launch your indie business, you'll want to do some basic calculations concerning the money you need and the money your business should generate. Here are some important financial skills to master.

DETERMINE YOUR PERSONAL CASH NEEDS

One of the first things you'll need to figure out is how much it costs for you to live on a monthly basis. You can calculate that by creating a Cost of Living Budget. Here's a sample form.

COST OF LIVING BUDGET

Household expenses	
Rent	__________
Telephone	__________
Gas and electricity	__________
Cable and online services	__________
Other household expenses	__________
Food	
At home	__________
Out	__________
Personal items	__________
Clothing	__________
Personal care items	
Publications	__________
Gifts	__________
Monthly payments	
Health insurance	__________
Student loan	__________
Car payments	__________
Other insurance	__________
Total	__________

In our example, Joseph determined that his monthly living expenses were approximately $800. His first cost of living budget looked like this.

JOSEPH D.'S COST OF LIVING BUDGET

Household expenses	
Rent	$ 200 (has three roommates)
Telephone	$ 40
Gas and electricity	$ 20
Cable and online services	$ 15
Other household expenses	$ 20
Food	
At home	$ 100
Out	$ 40
Personal Items	
Clothing	$ 50
Personal care items	$ 30
Entertainment	$ 60
Publications	$ 10
Gifts	$ 20
Monthly payments	
Health insurance	$ 100
Student loan	N/A
Car payments	$ 75
Savings/reserve	$ 20
Total	$ 800

After two months of being in business, however, Joseph realized his business could afford to pay him only $725 per month. He quickly revised his cost of living budget by cutting back on some of his personal expenses; he reduced his spending on eating out, entertainment, publications, and savings to fit his $725 income. Joseph's second cost of living budget looked like this:

JOSEPH D.'S LEAN and MEAN COST OF LIVING BUDGET

Household expenses	
Rent	$ 200 (has three roommates)
Telephone	$ 40
Gas and Eelectricity	$ 20
Cable and online services	$ 15
Other household expenses	$ 20
Food	
At home	$ 100
Out	$ 25
Personal Items	
Clothing	$ 25
Personal care items	$ 30
Entertainment	$ 20
Publications	$ 15
Gifts	$ 20
Monthly payments	
Health insurance	$ 100
Student loan	N/A
Car payments	$ 75
Savings/reserve	$ 20
Total	$ 725

Your cost of living budget will tell you the amount of money you need to get by on a monthly basis. You can decide how you plan to generate that income. You can do what Joseph did—count on your indie business to pay the bills—or you can find other sources of income while you build your indie venture. Here are several strategies for money management while building an indie business.

Save The Startup Money

Suzy D. was passionate about saving money. She worked throughout college, managing to save $10,000. After graduation, she temped full time as a legal proofreader while building her interior design business on the weekends. By the time Suzy was ready to open her own interior design company, she had $25,000 in savings for her personal use. Suzy liked knowing she could live off the $25,000 for one year while she focused on obtaining new clients.

Buy An Existing Company

Julia P. worked as a full-time photographer for an international photo stock company. She had a good relationship with the owners of the company, an elderly married couple. She also liked having a place to report to on a daily basis. Julia cultivated her relationship with the stock company owners with the intention of buying their business once they retired. Five years later, Julia was able to buy the business. The couple helped her get loans from financial institutions and agreed to stay on part time for one year to teach her more about running the business.

Go Into Partnership With A Financial Backer

Dennis C. was trained as an architect. He worked part time drafting for a prestigious architectural firm while he developed his own product—an ecologically safe home. After he spent one year researching, designing, and building models of his product, Dennis approached the head of the firm with his idea. The firm president liked Dennis' idea and agreed to back him financially. Within two years, they'd formed a business partnership and erected the first ecologically safe home in Kansas.

All of these examples illustrate different ways of making money to pay living expenses while developing an indie business idea. Your indie business idea should include a financial plan that includes concrete ways to meet your living expenses while you grow your business.

Many indies develop a service business first, because it is a much less expensive proposition. Once they establish a good reputation and turn a profit, they use their earnings to launch their product business. Whatever kind of business you want to start, find out how much it will cost to get it going.

KNOW YOUR STARTUP COSTS

Startup costs are the expenses involved in launching your indie idea. For service businesses, the startup costs tend to be low because you're selling expertise, not things. There are many kinds of service businesses: training, tutoring, counseling, cleaning, consulting, temping, designing, programming, writing, organizing. They all involve skills that you sell to clients at an hourly, daily, weekly, monthly, or project rate. Joseph sold his technical writing skills to his first client at a rate of $1,000 a month.

For product businesses, the startup costs tend to be higher because you have to produce the item you're selling first before you open your business. If your indie business involves a product like clothing, furniture, medical supplies, or hardware, you'll have to pay product-related expenses. Product startup costs include paying for the development of a prototype, buying raw materials, manufacturing the product, storing unsold or unshipped goods, and applying for a trademark or patent.

Startup costs for all indie ventures include things like stationery, business cards, file cabinets, telephone installation, directory listings, office space, office equipment, office supplies, insurance, and professional services (accountants, lawyers, etcetera).

Here's what Joseph's startup costs looked like.

Joseph D.'s Startup Costs

Stationery	$ 40
Business cards	$ 40
File cabinets	$ 25 (secondhand)
Telephone installation	N/A
Directory listing	$ 25
Office space	(working from home)
Office equipment	(already purchased computer)
Office supplies	$ 25
Insurance	N/A
Professional services	$ 175*
Total	$ 330

* Met with lawyer to get a legal contract form for clients and met with accountant to set up record keeping/

To estimate your indie venture's startup costs accurately, you can take advantage of reliable resources. You can go to your industry's trade association for information concerning the cost of doing business. You can also consult with an accountant or meet with someone already established in your industry. Wherever you get the assistance, calculating your startup costs accurately will be an important step in planning your indie business.

KNOW THE COST OF RUNNING YOUR BUSINESS

Every indie needs to know how much money it costs to run his or her business. Your operating expenses are everything you pay to keep the doors of your indie venture open. Operating expenses include such things as your salary, office rent (if applicable), utilities, telephone, insurance, postage, advertising and marketing, travel, employee salaries (if applicable), client entertainment, equipment rental, equipment repairs, office supplies, and professional services. If you have a product business, you'll have the additional expenses of producing, storing, and distributing your product.

As with startup costs, your best bet is to enlist the advice of reliable experts for this information. Trade associations, accountants, bookkeepers, and/or experienced indies in your industry can help you estimate what your operating expenses are likely to be.

Joseph's monthly operating expenses for the first six months of his business were as follows:

Joseph D.'s Operating Expenses

Joseph's salary	$ 725
Office rent	
Utilities	
Telephone	
Office supplies	$ 20
Postage	$ 20
Travel	
Advertising/marketing	$ 35
Client entertainment	
Equipment rental	
Equipment repairs	
Professional services	
Insurance	
Taxes	$ 200
Total	$1,000

Unlike Joseph, you'll want to estimate the cost of running your indie venture *before* you start business. It will prepare you in several ways:

- You'll know how much money you'll need every month to keep your indie venture going.
- You'll know how much money you need to make (how many units of your product or service you need to sell) just to break even.
- You can prepare a reserve of money (using savings or a loan) to keep you afloat while you pursue your first pieces of business.

KNOW YOUR INDUSTRY'S PAYMENT PRACTICES

As you begin planning your indie career, there are two important questions you want to answer:

- What fee should I charge for my product or service?
- How should I expect to be paid?

The answers will depend on what industry you're in.

Determining Your Fee

The first question, "What fee should I charge for my product or service?" is very important because your price will directly influence your ability to make money as an indie.

(Price × Number of units sold) — Operating Expenses = Profit

Setting a price is often frightening for new indies. The tendency is to set a very low price in hopes of beating the competition. The problem is that lower prices don't necessarily lead to higher sales. If you underprice your product or service, potential customers may assume that you're selling something of low quality.

Smart indies do preliminary research before they set a price for their service or product. They find out what other people charge for similar goods. Eventually, they establish a fee structure which incorporates their business' costs and compares well with the competition.

Knowing How You Will Be Paid

The second question, "How should I expect to be paid?" can be answered by studying the standard methods of payment within your industry. Joseph learned the hard way that it is common for technical writers to be paid 30 days after billing their clients. A retail store owner can expect immediate payment for any items he or she sells.

You can find out the standard payment practices within your industry by speaking with other indies in your line of work. Trade associations are also excellent resources for this information.

Once you find out how and when you will get paid, you can implement your own procedures to insure swift payment. Here are some billing practices that all indies need to adhere to:

1. Have a clearly defined payment schedule for every client or customer.
2. Bill clients regularly and follow up on late payers.
3. Do not do business with people who consistently argue over your fees or fail to pay for work you've already delivered.

ADVANCED STRATEGIES PART I: THE PSYCHOLOGY OF ASKING FOR MONEY

The ability to talk to customers, clients, and vendors about money is critical for small business success. Unfortunately, asking for money or discussing fees is often an emotionally charged activity, bringing up personal questions of self-worth, competence, cordiality, and value.

The most common psychological defense against dealing with the issue of money is vagueness. The fantasy is that if you remain vague on the topic of money, you will avoid rejection and/or confrontation. In reality, until you clarify for yourself and others the terms of your relationship, you jeopardize your own financial well-being.

Tax Update

One of the challenges of working for yourself is doing the taxes for your business. You'll need to keep on top of changes in the tax code. (Remember, you should always consult a tax professional to help you with your taxes.) The following U.S. income tax tips come from Jake Meyer, CPA.

For tax year 1996, if you are self-employed, you may deduct an amount equal to 30% of the payments you made for medical insurance on your individual tax return. This percentage will increase to 40% in 1997, 45% in years 1998-2002.

In 1996, salaried individuals will have social security tax witheld from the first $62,700 of income, only. This amount will increase to $65,400 for 1997. Medicare insurance will continue to be witheld from all wages.

Keep the meter running. The standard mileage rate for any business use of your car is 31 cents; 12 cents for mileage incurred in charitable work; and 10 cents for mileage incurred in the course of medical work. (Driving to doctor's appointments, for example.)

And keep those receipts! The threshold for employers and employees needing to provide documentation on most business expenses is $75. For business expenses of $75 or more, you'll need to be ready to back up your numbers with receipts or paid bills.

On your individual tax return, charitable donations of $250 or more must be substantiated by a written acknowledgement from the donee organization.

On the home front: You will need correct social security numbers for all children and other dependents on your individual tax return. If you don't provide the correct social security number, then your refund may be delayed and you may lose the benefit of the exemption. Employment taxes for wages paid to household employees during 1996 must be reported and paid with your individual income tax return.

In 1996, the amount of tangible business property that may be written off as an expense is $17,500. This amount will increase incrementally over the next few tax years. In 1997, the limit for business property expense will rise to $18,000.

Simple ways to gain clarity in your financial transactions:

- Find out what your potential client's budget is first. If it's far below your standard fee, look for greener pastures.

- Before starting work, make sure the financial terms of your agreement are crystal clear and spelled out in writing.

- Investigate the payment history of a large corporation. Past payment behavior is a good indication of how you will be treated.

- When discussing your fees, have a price list with you for backup.

- When dealing with vendors, come up with your budget first—know how much you can realistically pay for their product or service. Ask for a written estimate.

- Above all, if you find it difficult to negotiate financial agreements in your business, get support. Draw on the experience of other business owners to write proposals, ask for money, raise prices, etcetera. Use an accountant or financial advisor to clarify your financial needs.

ADVANCED STRATEGIES PART II: DEALING WITH DEADBEATS

Small business owners and freelancers share a big problem: collecting money from deadbeat clients. Here are some tips for beating this business hazard.

- Stay on top of your receivables. Review them every week. Take action whenever necessary.

- When faced with a client who is late in payment, react immediately. If your policy is to receive payment within 30 days, call on day 30. Deadbeat clients usually only respond to those who push for the check.

- Have your fee and payment agreement written up and signed by the payer.

- Call and send invoices frequently; keep the payer aware of your presence.

- Refuse more business until the old business is paid for.

- Don't lower an agreed-upon fee for the promise of future business. This rarely works and leaves you feeling more ripped off than before.
- If possible, charge interest for invoices that remain unpaid beyond a cutoff date.
- If necessary, contact a collection agency to get your money.
- Stay calm. Be professional but consistent.
- Stay firm and confident.
- Be clear and up front about the money.
- Never avoid talking about finances.

chapter 20
COMMITMENT

> "Big shots are only little shots who keep shooting."
> Christopher Morley

Robert W. was determined to start a dating service. No obstacle could stand in his way. He didn't have the money for advertising. He didn't have the computer software he needed. He didn't even have enough male partners for the women he knew were interested. None of these obvious problems stopped Robert. He was committed to making his idea become a reality.

Through hard work and persistent action, Robert found ways to make his indie venture happen. First, he got free publicity for his business by convincing local radio and television shows to interview him about "Dating In The Nineties." Then, Robert joined a business barter group and secured the services of an excellent computer programmer who could set up the software for his dating service. Finally, Robert found the single men he needed by approaching men's health clubs. He constructed a deal with the clubs whereby they would offer men free enrollment in the dating service as a special membership privilege.

Within four months, Robert's dating service was up and running. His drive and commitment made it possible for him to override the obstacles he faced, and create the business of his dreams.

Successful indies like Robert commit to doing whatever it takes to get their venture off the ground. They commit to persevering for however long it takes. It's common knowledge among established indies that most businesses take more time and more effort than we imagine to launch successfully. We hit unanticipated obstacles as we pursue our goals. But delays and obstacles are not sound reasons for giving up.

DRIVE, WHAT FUELS COMMITMENT

Without drive, a good indie idea usually goes no further than the thinking stage. Drive leads to initiative, innovation, taking actions, taking risks. Indies need drive to keep them moving through the obstacles and delays that are inherent in pursuing an independent business venture. In Robert's case, his drive helped him find solutions to each roadblock he encountered on the way to launching his dating service.

Drive is not something you can learn. For instance, there are no courses given in college on how to develop drive. But drive is available to each one of us when we want something badly enough. In fact, you've already used drive to achieve some of your academic, social, and creative goals. Common activities that require drive include:

- going out for a sports team
- auditioning for performing arts
- applying for a scholarship
- striving for excellence as an athlete
- entering a creative competition
- winning awards for mastery of a skill
- raising money for good causes

Have you used drive to pursue any of these activities? When have you felt so driven to accomplish something that nothing got in your way?

Why Indies Need Drive and Commitment

Having drive and commitment enables indies to weather the ups and downs in business. Nothing in life is good all of the time. If things were always good, we wouldn't need commitment. Yet some people take the tough times as a signal to quit their indie business. As you practice commitment with your indie enterprise, you'll realize that its the *process* of reaching your goals that adds value to your life—not just the winning. Commitment adds character to you and your business, because commitment helps you work through problems and grow.

John W.'s tenth shipment of coffee was scheduled to arrive momentarily from South America. Unfortunately, he hadn't presold enough orders to pay for the shipping. The first nine shipments of coffee were easier to sell. John secured orders from most of the retail stores he contacted. This time, two years later, some of his original customers had gone out of business and some had begun buying from John's competitors. It was difficult for John to find new customers and he'd become lax about pursuing them. Rather than make the effort to sell this shipment of coffee, John considered abandoning it or having it sent back to South America.

John W.'s story illustrates how a lack of commitment can jeopardize an indie business. Because John's imported coffee became a little more difficult to sell, he lost momentum. Unless John recommits to having a successful coffee import business, his indie venture will go down the drain.

A COMMITMENT QUIZ

Are you a committed person? In which areas of your life are you most able to practice commitment? Take the following quiz and see how you rate. (1= always, 5 = never)

Friends

I consistently keep the commitments I make to my friends.

Always Never

1 2 3 4 5

I try to resolve conflicts with my friends because I am committed to building the friendship.

Always Never

1 2 3 4 5

When someone becomes my friend, I stick by him/her through thick and thin.

Always Never

1 2 3 4 5

Family

I am committed to maintaining a good relationship with my family.

Always Never

1 2 3 4 5

If there is a conflict between me and a family member, I try to resolve it.

Always Never

1 2 3 4 5

I stand by my family members during good and bad times.

Always | | | | Never
1 | 2 | 3 | 4 | 5

School

I am committed to completing my formal education.

Always | | | | Never
1 | 2 | 3 | 4 | 5

I give time and energy to my school work, even when it is difficult.

Always | | | | Never
1 | 2 | 3 | 4 | 5

I am willing to do whatever it takes to do my best at school.

Always | | | | Never
1 | 2 | 3 | 4 | 5

Hobbies

I have a hobby to which I commit my time and energy.

Always | | | | Never
1 | 2 | 3 | 4 | 5

I keep pursuing my hobby, even when it isn't convenient.

Always | | | | Never
1 | 2 | 3 | 4 | 5

Sports

I commit a certain amount of time every week to sports.

Always | | | | Never
1 | 2 | 3 | 4 | 5

I give my time and energy to a specific sport on a regular basis.

Always | | | | Never
1 | 2 | 3 | 4 | 5

I am willing to do the work it takes to get good at my favorite sport.

Always — Never

1 2 3 4 5

Your ideas

I stand behind my ideas, even if other people think they are weird or goofy.

Always — Never

1 2 3 4 5

When I have a good idea, I am committed to making it happen. (e.g., if I have the idea to raise money via a bake sale, I actually make it happen).

Always — Never

1 2 3 4 5

I am willing to do whatever it takes to turn my ideas into reality.

Always — Never

1 2 3 4 5

Score

Add up all of your responses. If you scored 17–35 you are a *naturally committed person.* It is fairly easy for you to commit to the people and projects in your life. If you scored 36–62 you are probably a *conditionally committed person.* That means you can commit to certain people or projects on the condition that they really matter to you. If you scored 63–85 you are a *commitment-shy person.* Commitments don't come easily or naturally to you. Commitment-shy people need to start making small commitments to themselves on a regular basis so that they can build this skill.

Commitment and drive are difficult to measure. You'll know you're committed to something when you can keep pursuing it, even when difficulties arise. You'll know you have drive when you find ways to reach your goals no matter what obstacles you face. Both of these internal qualities will benefit you as an indie.

By practicing commitment and drive, you'll experience the rewards of perseverance and resourcefulness. You'll be able to weather the ups and downs that all smart indies know are a necessary part of ultimate success.

chapter 21

ADVICE FROM REAL INDIES

STEFAN KILLEN,
Graphic Designer

Where did you go to school?

Evergreen State College. It's in Olympia, Washington. It's one of those alternative schools from the sixties. No grades, no exams.

What did you graduate with?

A B.A. That's all they give. They don't have majors per se. I studied mainly liberal arts. If I majored in anything it was fine arts, drawing, and painting.

Did you intern while you were in college?

Yes. The summer after my first year I found this internship with a government agency that was being offered, unpaid. I interviewed with them. They were interested. I had an interview with another agency on the same day—a film library. They paid but it was in the basement of this building and I just couldn't do it. I didn't want to work in a basement all summer. So I ran back to the first place and I said, "Can you give me $5 an hour?" and they said, "O.K." So I did that for a summer and then that fall we turned it into a two-day-a-week thing. For four years, I worked for them full time during the summer, two days a week during the year.

What did you learn there?

I got into it right when computers were starting. The first year I learned cutting and pasting and so on. After a year, I started to work on computers.

So, you were doing graphic design?

Yes, but there was no design department. I was just helping the P.R. person and teaching myself everything there was to know. When I started, they said, "Do you know anything about graphic design?" I said, "Well, I studied art, so I can learn." I convinced them that I could do the job.

After a year and a half or two years, they asked me to work on a freelance basis with them. That was the beginning of my freelance career.

How did they differentiate between an internship and a freelance position?

It had to do with taxes primarily. As freelance, I had to deal with my own taxes.

So, when you were an intern, the state agency dealt with your taxes?

Yes. So basically, I fell into that. I had no training or experience in graphic design; no desire to be a graphic designer. I just had an arts background throughout my life. I had done some graphic design in high school with the school newspaper.

I kept doing it because it paid better than most of the jobs my friends had, and I kept upping my fees from $5 per hour to $7 to $10 to $12 per hour. And, after I graduated, I kept working there, at the government agency, freelance for 30 hours a week for two years. Thirty hours was my choice because I wanted to do other stuff.

Then I left the west coast and moved to New York. I didn't have a job when I moved. I found a job through the *New York Times* working at a public relations company as an assistant designer. The software I was using at the time was Ventura Publisher, an IBM-based program. It wasn't the first choice of programs for designers, but it was pretty good.

The head designer for the company quit two months after I got there. I became art director. I stayed a year and a half and learned a lot. I hadn't worked with people before then at all. I'd been completely on my own in the state agency.

Once you were promoted to art director, you stayed there for a year and a half. Then what happened?

Then I started thinking about leaving and hooked up with a man who worked at a publishing house who was looking for a freelancer to come in-house on a limited basis. He agreed to give me a minimum of two days of work each week. I did my math and figured I could pay my bills on that assignment. And I would try to come up with other work to supplement my income. As it turned out, they kept giving me more work. It became four days a week.

So, you didn't need other clients?

No. I didn't. It was pretty much subsistence living. I wasn't living the high life. But it was enough for what I wanted and expected at the time. That was three and a half years ago. I've kept that client ever since. Things have changed. I'm no longer working on-site at all. I could, but I'm choosing to work at my own office. I have other clients now.

At what point did you start acquiring other clients?

Basically, when I started taking your seminar this summer with Katherine Crowley. Three years later.

I actually had a couple of other clients. That company split into two, so then I had two clients. Then, Buddhist friends of mine contacted me and that became a third client. And then a former V.P. at the public relations place who had also quit shortly after I left contacted me and became a fourth client. And there were a few small assignments here and there. But basically work came my way; I didn't lift a finger to get work for three years.

Then I decided it was time to start taking a little more charge directing where I was going. Things like upping my rates and contacting potential clients.

So this one client started your business, and now you have a business?

Yes.

Do you have any advice for someone coming out of college?

Internships are a good way to go. But one thing I did not do was work with other graphic designers. My learning curve in terms of graphic design and money and everything has been slower than it could have been because I didn't have other designers to learn from. I did my best at copying ideas and teaching myself, but I think that for me it's a valuable thing to have someone look at my work and give advice or feedback.

I recommend getting internships with graphic designers who can teach you, train you, give you feedback. It's both a way to learn and a way to get energies and ideas about the business. Today, I feel more interested in what I'm doing because this summer I shifted into higher gear. I've been interacting with other designers on some jobs. I'm choosing to care more about what I do and to identify myself a little more as a graphic designer.

So there's been some ambivalence?

Yes.

Do you know what changed the ambivalence?

For a long time I kept saying, "Well, I'm doing this for today, and we'll wait and see." That's still the attitude I have. I still don't feel like I'm going to do this for the rest of my life. But I do feel like since I'm still doing it, I want to do it more professionally. I want to be better at what I'm doing. I want to make more money at what I'm doing. I think that operating on a really small scale made graphic design as a profession a frustrating thing. I didn't have a second phone line for a fax machine. I didn't have a strong computer, scanner, or printer. Details like that make operating a business easier.

Other than keeping yourself small and that being frustrating, is there anything else you would have done differently?

I don't think so. All along I went where there were options and possibilities. And that was good enough for a long time.

Actually, it sounds like a very indie career path.

The one real regret that I've had is not working with other graphic designers. In addition to the shared expertise, it's just a lot more fun to be around other people and bounce ideas off them.

DENISE CARUSO,
Milliner (Hat Designer) and Showroom Owner

Did you graduate from college?

No, I actually don't have a degree. But I went to college for many years. I studied business at the University of Texas, and then fashion at Parsons School of Design, and accessories at F.I.T. (the Fashion Institute of Technology).

When did your career officially start? Did you work through college?

Yes. I've always had to work.

So, you worked for money.

Yes.

Because some people work just for information . . .

I did that too. I interned at Betsey Johnson, which was purely for information. I interned at the Millinery Information Bureau. Actually, since I've been in New York, I pretty much didn't work for money. Before that I always worked for money.

So, while you were in New York studying fashion, you interned.

Yes.

Why didn't you graduate from any of these fashion schools?

I never could stay within my program. I didn't go to school for a degree. I went to school to get the knowledge to start a business. I already had a business in Texas. I made clothing for topless dancers. I did nightclub clothing. Dresses with marabou trim and cutouts on the side—discowear.

You made costumes.

Exactly.

You did that while you were in college?

I did that after attending college in Texas. I was 21 to 25 years old when I did that.

Did you sell to stores or just customers?

To the clubs. I went into the topless bars and would set up in the dressing rooms. It was very lucrative. But you had to spend all your time in a topless bar dressing room.

How did you get into that?

My Dad owns topless bars. So there you go.

So then you decided . . .

I decided I didn't really want to sell clothes in a topless bar. That wasn't really what I was after. I wanted to make clothing that was still fun but more serious than costumes. I knew how to sew. I bought patterns and I would alter them. I really wanted to learn how to design my own patterns.

So, I moved to Dallas and I started fashion school there and I hated it. It was very restricting. The teacher would say, "Do 15 lingerie sketches." I would say, "I don't want to do lingerie." She would say, "You have to." Then I'd design pajamas and the teacher would say, "This isn't lingerie." I fought all the time.

So, then I decided to move to New York City to go to Parsons. I came here and went to school. I went to Parsons first for two and a half years, and then I went to F.I.T. for a year.

And it was during those years that you got internships.

Yes.

Then what happened? Did any of your internships turn into hiring situations?

No. I could have worked at Betsey Johnson. But I pretty much got everything I was ever going to learn there during my internship. So, I was studying fashion design, and I didn't get a degree at Parsons because I was all over the place. I took courses like Designing a Retail Image, press classes, photography classes. I didn't stay within my plan so I didn't get a degree. I didn't care about it. I have never cared about it. I mean, what does it matter as long as you have the intelligence and the knowledge you need? No one has ever asked me for a piece of paper. I've never said I graduated from anywhere.

Okay, then what happened? How did you get your business idea?

I was taking a millinery course as an elective. It was really fun and also it was very instantaneous. One of the things I hate about clothing is you sketch it, then you make a pattern, then you have to sew it. It's very long and drawn out. And I'm great with beginning things, but I hate detail and I don't like continuing . . .

You like instant gratification.

Exactly. Hats are instant gratification. So then I went to F.I.T. and started taking some hat classes. And I figured, 'You know, it's a lot easier to start a hat company than it is to start a clothing company.' To do a clothing company you have to spend a lot of money just to put out one piece of clothing. It's like a thousand bucks to produce and package one tank top. I didn't have that kind of money and hats were a lot easier to do. They were also very "hot" at the time I started.

So, when I was still at school, at Parsons, I took a course where the class project was to design a line. The teacher was really great and she let me do hats. I designed a line of hats, and the teacher took them to Bloomingdale's and they bought them. Then, I took them to Bendel's and they bought them. That experience was both good and bad because it gave me the idea that you just take stuff to stores and they buy it. It's a lot harder than that.

I just happened to hit it very lucky at the beginning. And, I sold the same hats to a couple of boutiques here in New York. After that, I went to F.I.T. and really studied hats for a year. When I finished with the year, I put together a line and started selling wholesale.

Would you do anything differently if you had it to do again?

Yes, I would. I think I would work for someone first. When you're in school, people always tell you that you should work for people because it's better to learn on their money than it is to learn on your money. However, when I was in school, nobody ever told me that. They just said, "You can do it. Go ahead. Go ahead." But really, even if you're the most gifted person in the world, you still should work for other people because there are so many things about the industry that you won't learn as quickly by yourself.

I worked for a jewelry designer when I got out of school for a while. I learned a lot from him too.

What was it like for you during the early stages of opening your business? Did you ever have moments of thinking "What am I doing?"

Oh, sure. I still have them. Because when you run your own business you have to be willing to give up everything. Your business has to become your number one priority. So you have no social life, you have no financial life. Everything goes into the business. I still wonder all the time. I could get a job making decent money. Go to work every day and when you leave, you leave.

But then I think about the bosses I've had and the jobs I've had. I start reading the classifieds and say, "oh, no."

So, a job is not really viable for you?

I don't think so. Everybody in my family is entrepreneurial. Nobody ever went to work. They always had businesses. Everyone was active. My grandmother owned a motel. My other grandmother owned an antique store. So, everybody had their own business. It's pretty much all I know.

Do you ever desire to be employed?

Only for the financial stability. Also, I really like press and marketing. It would be really nice to work with somebody who had a sizable budget. Then I could really do something as opposed to working with my marketing budget, which is nothing.

Tell me more about the evolution of your business.

I've been designing hats about three and a half years. For the first couple of years, I kept designing the hats. I kept building my customer base. And then I was going to share a space with a friend of mine because I needed to move my business out of my house and get a showroom space.

You'd been operating your business out of your house?

Yes. I was selling hats wholesale from my home in New Jersey. And I had a showroom in New York to represent the line. They would do the sales and the marketing. Through that time, I had some hard times. I was sick for a while. I had to get a job with a jewelry designer to supplement my income.

I worked with him for a year and a half. That was a really good experience because he made $1.5 million a year, and ran his business out of a two-person office. So it was really good to see how to keep your overhead down, and that you can really run a tight ship. So many people in the garment industry operate from an "excess is everything," "image is everything," attitude. So they have big showrooms and staff when they can't really afford it.

He was really low key. It was good to see that kind of business. For this jewelry designer, I basically did everything. I was his assistant. I did the shipping, the credit checking, sales, marketing plans. That was a really good experience. All this time, I'm still doing my hats. Still growing my business.

When it came time to find my own space, I was going to share it with a friend. We rented it together and then she pulled out. I was left with a very big space on Fifth Avenue. Because I'm really good with press and marketing, I had always in the back of my mind wanted to have a showroom where designers could show their goods, and it wasn't driven by the bottom line. Everyone could be more creative. Maybe the sales wouldn't be as huge, but you could still keep the integrity of who you are, and everyone could make a living.

So, I started putting ads in newspapers announcing that I was looking for designers who wanted to rent space in my showroom and display their lines to potential buyers. It's been a year, I have fifteen lines now. Everybody pays me a showroom fee. I get commissions on the sales I make.

Do you like this better?

Sometimes. I really like the press and marketing part. That's my favorite part of the business, even more than the designing. I really seem to have a knack for it. I can get things in magazines, on T.V. If I set a goal of getting a press clip in some magazine, I usually accomplish it. That's kind of nice.

Do you think there are more businesses in you?

Oh yes. Definitely. I have things already that I would like to do that are more stable. I like to launch things and then leave them. I'm good with the big ideas and I hate the details.

Do you have any advice for someone in college now?

Yes: Intern. Pick somewhere that would be your dream job. Even though you don't make any money, spend the time there. You get to see how the business works. What you learn in school is probably very very far removed from how a business actually works.

When you're in school, you think fashion is very glamorous. But, when you go and see the contractors making the clothes, you know it's not. When you're in the back room dressing models you see it's a lot of hard work. Hands-on experience really gives you a better perspective of how hard people work in the industry, and how fastpaced it is.

SUZANNE SWIFT,
Owner of InfoEdge and SpecSimple Computer Information Systems

Did you work in high school?

I tried to start a business tutoring other high school students for the SAT and had no takers.

You put up fliers and nobody responded?

I got the idea from a friend I went to music school with. He and a friend of his seemed to have a successful business tutoring students for the SAT. I brought together two people who'd gotten in early admission to Harvard and two people who'd gotten in early admission to Yale, passed around flier, and tried to get parents interested. Nobody expressed any interest.

I also worked for Toys-R-Us for two weeks during high school. Between high school and college, I worked for a title insurance company doing administrative work. I worked for a toy store one summer in college and freelanced as a percussionist all during college.

When did you know that you wanted to start a business?

It's my natural inclination. I've always started businesses. I don't know that I ever thought concretely, 'I'm starting a business. I'm going to put my name up on a building somewhere. I'm going to get letterhead and stationery.' It was never a plan, exactly. I would simply start something that other people wanted me to do for them.

I started making thread bracelets for people when I was eight years old during summer camp. I made some very intricate designs. People liked them, so I started charging a dollar a bracelet. I made up swatch cards so customers could see all the different combinations. Then I'd stay up until two or three in the morning weaving bracelets, filling orders for that day. In the morning, I'd go in, tie them on people's wrists, make them happy, get more orders, and then go back at night and fill orders.

Would you say you liked the money-making aspect of it or you just liked the work?

I liked the work. I liked the fact that I was making money.

Would you have done it if you weren't making money?

Probably not in the same context. The money was a motivating factor. Having money in the bank always felt good. When I was a kid, I always saved. Everything I earned went into my bank account. Watching my bank account grow was exciting.

You went to college for what?

I had a liberal arts education. I studied Chinese. I studied Chinese History. At the end of my junior year, I decided I wanted to be an architect, so in my senior year I changed my whole course structure. I didn't graduate with a degree in architecture, but managed to combine China and architecture by doing a thesis on ancient Chinese architecture. After graduation, I spent a year in China.

What did you think you were going to do at that point?

During senior year everyone seemed to be looking for jobs. The investment banks came to school to interview students and I remember asking the director of Career Services, "Should I just go in for an interview?" She warned me not to. She said, "You've got to really want this. Don't go in to interview with banks because if you get it and don't want it, you take the place of someone who does (want it)." So I didn't go on any bank interviews.

The only thing I knew was that I wanted to live in China. I had studied Chinese for many years. I had studied Chinese history, economics, and politics, and I wanted to experience China for myself. I thought it was really, really important to see what I'd studied up close. And it was. It was vital. Living in China gave me a completely different perspective than I'd had as a student.

When you got close to the end of that year, what did you think you were going to do?

As a senior I'd applied for what Yale calls "externships." Externships take place during spring break. Students apply for an externship with a company that has Yale alumnae. I applied for an externship in architecture and I got it. I was really amazed because I had very little architecture experience. The other architecture students weren't too happy with me. I got it because I had a diverse background.

How is an externship different from an internship?

It's the same thing. I worked at an architecture firm for two weeks and became good friends with the woman who hired me. When I got back from China, I called up my friend and asked, "Do you have any openings?" My friend questioned whether I was sure I wanted to go into architecture because she was considering leaving the field. When I said I was, she told me, "There's an opening, come on in and talk to the partners." So I went in and they hired me on the spot. I worked there for about six months.

What was your job there?

I was a design apprentice. At first I dimensioned buildings. I was in charge of dimensioning this huge building in the Wall Street area. Two other interns and I dimensioned every floor of a sixteen floor building. We measured, then we drew up plans.

Did you like that?

It was fun. In retrospect, it was brainless work. But the very first time doing it was exciting. The responsibility, the pressure of a deadline, and meeting the deadline felt exciting.

In architecture, there is a feeling of dedication to an art. I didn't worry about getting paid for the exact number of hours I'd worked. I just wanted all the experience I can possibly get. So, I probably would have worked for nothing.

Were they paying you?

Yes. They paid me.

Did they pay you during the internship?

I think they gave me a stipend. Not much. Just enough to cover lunch and transportation.

So you're doing this measuring. Then what happened?

My mentor who'd brought me in on the internship became really sick. She was out for a month, and eventually left the company. She had brought me in so my position with management was not very strong.

Compounding that, I'd studied architecture theory at Yale, but didn't know any technique. I was not from a tech school where they taught you the "right" way to draft. I picked things up quickly, but started from square one with many of the basics like lettering and drafting. I really needed a stronger background as they were paying me to do those things.

While I learned quickly, management had a different perception of what I should know as a Yale graduate. The thing I learned the quickest: Autocad. I made the Autocad operators very nervous because I was being paid a lot less than they were.

I got "laid off" after six months.

Were you disappointed?

I was crushed. I'd never been booted from a job before. I didn't like the management, so I wasn't truly sad to be moving on. I felt they never really screened me adequately to determine what my skills were, and they gave me no training. I learned Autocad on my own time, at night.

You worked way beyond what they expected?

No question.

This is an important indie characteristic.

I would work until midnight every night, practicing Autocad.

So, in a way, you got a lot out of the firm. They didn't get that much out of you . . .

Exactly. Well, they did get a lot out of me on my first project—the Wall Street building we measured. It went very smoothly and everyone was impressed. Then the guy who'd brought in that piece of business left. In the end, everyone I respected and liked was gone.

It became an issue of office politics. Office politics was a real eye opener. It left a bitter taste because it was something I felt I had no control over. How can you be nice to people you really don't respect and don't like? My personality was too rigid, and I really just couldn't overcome my distaste.

So then what happened?

The firm was actually very good to me. They gave me the number of a furniture dealership they worked with who they knew had an opening. It wasn't something that they had to do, but one of the partners and I got along very well and so he made a call.

A couple of days later I had this interview with the furniture dealership. They were thrilled with me. Rattled from my architecture experience, I felt I had to redeem myself. I pretty much took the first job that came along.

In retrospect, I don't know what I would have done otherwise. I guess I would have gone back to school if I truly felt I wanted to be an architect. But I wasn't convinced. I figured, working with a furniture dealership would let me see what other architecture firms were like. And then I'd find out if my unpleasant experience was typical of the industry. Maybe there were other firms out there that were better. At least that was my rationale for taking the job.

My new job was in the library. I was hired to run a design resource library that was open to architects and designers. The library had a reputation of being top-notch but had fallen into disarray. They hired me and I got the place back on its feet.

What did they hire you for?

My job title was resource coordinator/specifications writer. Which meant I was to meet with industry representatives, keep the binders and samples up to date, and write a newsletter in-house so that everyone knew about industry changes. I was the point person for all questions about product and manufacturers.

Furniture dealerships are the middle men between manufacturers and the end-user. This particular company liked to describe themselves as the Cadillac of furniture dealerships. They did many projects with large corporations. They were a high-end firm in a low-end industry.

The furniture dealership hired me to do something that I had absolutely no background for. I walked into a job where I was expected to be an expert about furniture—a topic I knew nothing about. That turned out not to be a bad thing because I used my computer experience to build databases to keep track of the information. That was my way of training myself and it turned out to be the foundation of my business.

But I'm convinced that if I hadn't taken this job, if I'd gone anyplace else, I would have developed a niche and I would have found some way to start my own business. That's just the kind of person I am.

At the furniture dealership I ran into office politics again, which I really didn't enjoy. I think I needed to be softened up, and learn to work with people I normally wouldn't have had anything to say to. I had to learn to respect people for things other than their intelligence . . . which was hard.

How long were you there?

I was there about a year. Six months into my tenure, I came up with the concept for my business.

How did the concept come up?

It came up because I was supposed to be a furniture expert. And I had no clue. The company had a database program, and I began to create databases just to keep track of all the information. I would create these elaborate questionnaires that each representative had to fill out. "What kind of chair do you have?" and other questions like that so that I could generate any kind of specification instantaneously.

If someone came into the library and asked for a systems manufacturer at a low price point I had it. And I didn't have to know it.

Did the company like that?

Oh they loved it. They thought it was great. The partners loved me. They realized I wasn't too savvy with office politics, and they worked with me on that.

What went wrong with "politics?" Do you have a story about that?

I think I was probably a bit too hard-nosed. I instituted a Rep of the Month thing to make the reps work harder and most people laughed up their sleeves. "It'll never happen."

And then it did happen?

No, it didn't really. It fell through. It worked the first month and then quickly petered out. I would make changes in the library and I'd realize that people were unhappy with change. Unless you really paved the way very carefully and made them feel very comfortable with what the change was going to be, it wasn't wise to spring change on them.

So you were there how long, a year?

A year before I incorporated my business. The last six months I worked part-time.

So you got the idea within six months but kept your job?

I kept the job because I had to build my databases and I had to figure a way to formulate the business. A rep took me under his wing. He was someone who noticed what I was doing. He said, "Suzanne, why are you doing this just here? Why don't you make a business of it?"

We met over a period of six months, and he helped me formulate a business plan. He wanted a piece of the business but in the end, he didn't have the funding for it. He helped me clarify the plan, the ideas and the goals. He was really instrumental in getting me to think on a larger scale.

I had initially wanted to work with the furniture dealership. I wanted to show them the product, and then have them fund me. As it turned out, they were too smart for themselves. They thought that if they could get me to sign on as an employee with the things that I developed on my own that they could then take control of the whole business. It was a little hard for them to have a partnership with a 23 year old.

At that point I went my own way. Negotiations with the dealership took six months, back and forth. When I saw it was going nowhere, I left.

You tried to get them to buy your concept, to make you a partner?

Yes. They had funding, a huge financial backing. I had a computer, a printer, the guts, and the knowledge.

When they didn't offer me anything of substance, I left. I had two new dealerships lined up already, and had a third that came on board pretty quickly after that.

So you said, "Good-bye." Were you scared? Did you have enough business?

I had business. I had two accounts. It was just barely enough to keep me afloat.

You mean you didn't really need the funding?

There were two different things going on here. I have two different businesses. InfoEdge, which is a library maintenance company. And SpecSimple which is the Internet Website. SpecSimple is what I really wanted to do. I didn't have much interest in doing InfoEdge. But since InfoEdge was a money maker, I had to do it in order to be able to develop Spec Simple.

The clients I had lined up were all library maintenance jobs. The money they paid me enabled me to develop SpecSimple. That was the idea. InfoEdge was such an embryonic company that it really took me a year and a half to get comfortable with it and grow the business. It ate up all my time.

I'd gone into this business to get to this other business, and I wasn't ever getting to this other business. That didn't change until my partner Jim came into the picture and took over the technical aspects of SpecSimple.

So, you never actually go funding?

No. I funded it myself.

Sounds like it went pretty smoothly, your transition from the job to your own business . . .

It went smoothly on the surface. I was tense for a long time. I had to wait for a third client to come in before I knew I could pay my rent. I'd moved out of my parents' house and really didn't want to have to move back. So there was a period that was pretty nerve-wracking.

Actually, it was nerve-wracking for the whole first year and a half. It was a new business. It was something that I'd developed entirely on my own. I had no one to ask questions about how to shape the business, because I'd created it. I'd started from scratch on everything. And that's scary. You work on blind faith.

Did you ever think it wasn't going to work?

About half the time I wasn't sure that I was going to make it. I knew I would never give it up, but I wasn't sure that things would fly. And I think that fear only went away relatively recently. Over the past year, I could see the progress. I began to understand how my company's work fit with the work of other companies.

Do you have anything you would do differently?

Lots of things. Do you want it alphabetically or categorically?

How about top priorities. The number one thing you would do differently now?

I guess the most important thing I learned is how to communicate with my clients. My business was so new to me that it was hard to communicate about something that was continually changing. I've learned since how to communicate. How to hold meetings with people and discuss what's going on in the business and find out how you can fit inside their business and find out how your company can become more valuable to their company. I think that's probably the most important point.

I've learned that when you say you're going to do something, to always follow up. It's just so so so so critical. And it doesn't happen all the time. But when you do follow up, people are really happy and relieved and they know that they can trust you.

It's common sense. When you're starting a business, it's such an exhausting process. You don't have control of all the details. Probably the most important detail to have control over is communication with your customers.

You're talking about customer service?

Yes. For my particular business. For someone who's making widgets, maybe it's not.

Would you ever go back to a job?

I think about that from time to time. There was one point when I was thinking I wanted to do venture capitalism because then I could assess new businesses and help the strong ones get funding. But, right now that seems very far removed.

I'm so concerned with getting SpecSimple, our Website, up and successful. And I'm so concerned with how and if I can make it big (because I don't have the funding at this point).

When I started InfoEdge, I didn't need much to start. There was a very real need. With SpecSimple, it's a need people don't know they have. They can get the same kind of information any number of harder ways, but this way is so much easier. I need to train prospective customers and teach them how to use new technology in order to use SpecSimple. To do that you need advertising dollars, you need marketing, you need press. You need a lot of things. It's just business on an entirely different level.

If I remove myself from it, which I try to do, I just look at it as a business exercise. You do as much as you can. You do as good as you can. And it's all experience. Granted I'm not 23 anymore, I'm 27. But I still feel like I'm young enough to say that I'm just learning a whole lot of stuff. If it doesn't work for this particular company, there will always be another one.

If it means focusing and going back to work for somebody to learn the industry, before I then branch out on my own . . . I don't know if I'd ever go to work for somebody. I think I'd rather form a partnership—a bunch of people who all had different specialties who work together to form something big. I think it would only be in a technology-related field.

I think I'm beyond the mentoring stage. I could be wrong, but I think I'm beyond the stage of really needing that guidance and alliance. I learn very quickly just by looking out of the corner of my eye.

Do you have any advice for people just coming out of college?

You really have nothing to lose. You have age on your side, energy on your side. You've got new ideas and you're not inhibited by the business process. You can sometimes see more clearly, especially when it comes to new technology. And the rest of it you'll learn.

RESOURCES

Government

The **U.S. Business Advisor** Web site for one-stop access to federal government information services and transactions.

http://www.business.gov

The **Small Business Administration** (SBA) provides helpful free information and services. A particularly helpful service they offer is a toll-free hotline. Call if you have questions about SBA loans or need general small-business information. SBA Answer Desk: (800) 827-5722. Visit the SBA Web site (http://www.sba.gov) to connect with a host of services for small businesses.

The **National Small Business Development Center Research Network** (http://www.smallbiz.suny.edu) is another helpful Internet destination.

Looking for a mentor? Get in touch with **SCORE—the Service Corps of Retired Executives.** They are retired business owners who give free advice. You can find them through the SBA.

Small-Business Magazines Online

Inc. Magazine (http://www.inc.com) is a trove of information, listing thousands of articles.

Fast Company (http://www.fastcompany.com) debuted in 1996 to support emerging growth companies.

Entrepreneurial Magazine (http://www.edgeonline.com) is sponsored by the Edward Lowe Foundation.

Family Businesses

Net Marquee (http://www.nmq.com) is dedicated to family business issues.

Raising Capital

Indies and small business owners can let their fingers do the fund-raising at http://www.money-hunter.com.

Online Discussion Groups and Services

The **i village site** (http://www.aboutwork.com) is a virtual water cooler and more. Besides the chat discussion groups, i village provides many other useful and interesting services for small businesses.

The **idea cafe** (http://www.ideacafe.com) is the Internet's small business channel, a fun approach to serious business.

The **Let's Talk Business Network** (http://www.ltbn.com) is a small business online support community.

Working Solo (http://www.workingsolo.com) offers a variety of services and products for independent entrepeneurs.

Finally, here are toll-free numbers for some of the major online service providers.

America Online: (800) 827-3338
CompuServe: (800) 524-3388
eWorld: (800) 775-4556
The Microsoft Network: (800) 386-5550

Books

Bangs Jr., David H. *Managing by the Numbers: Financial Essentials for the Growing Business.* Upstart Publishing. Straightforward techniques for money management.

Bangs Jr., David H. *The Start-Up Guide: A One-Year Plan for Entrepreneurs.* Upstart Publishing.

Barker, Joel Arthur. *Paradigms.* HarperBusiness. Discover the future through this book.

Covey, Stephen R. *The 7 Habits of Highly Effective People.* Simon & Schuster. A step-by-step guide to achieving the human characteristics that really create success.

Edwards, Sarah and Paul. *Making It On Your Own.* St. Martin's Press. A comprehensive look at small-business isues from the practical to the psychological.

Gallagher, Bill, Wilson, Orval, Levinson, Jay. *Guerrilla Selling.* Houghton Mifflin. Excellent selling techniques.

Gates, Bill. *The Road Ahead.* Viking. The founder of Microsoft gives his vision of the future.

Hopkins, Tom. *How to Master The Art of Selling.* Warner Books. A master salesperson tells all.

Jaffe, Azriela. *Honey, I Want to Start My Own Business.* HarperBusiness. A guide for couples going into business together.

Popcorn, Faith. *Clicking.* HarperCollins. A futurist prognosticates on consumer trends.

Whitmyer, Claude, Raspberry, Salli. *Running A One-Person Business.* Gives a clear plan of action for being on your own.